10 STEPS TO SELF-LOVE

(HOW TO FALL IN LOVE WITH YOURSELF)

By Julia Roman

Copyright © 2022 Julia Roman

All rights reserved. No part of this publication may be shared, reproduced or transmitted in any electronic, digital or material form (including photocopying). The author asserts their moral rights to be identified as the author of this book. Images courtesy of Canva©

DISCLAIMER

This book has been written and published for informational and educational purposes only. It is not intended to serve as medical advice or to be any form of medical treatment. You should always consult your physician before altering or changing any aspect of your medical treatment. Any use of the information in this book is made on the reader's good judgment and is the reader's sole responsibility. This book is not intended to diagnose or treat any medical condition and is not a substitute for a physician. I am not a licensed medical health care professional. The purchaser or reader of this book assumes full responsibility of the use of the material and information. The author does not assume any responsibility for errors, omissions, or other interpretations of the subject matter. All names have been changed to respect the privacy of clients.

This book is dedicated to my beautiful mother Kathy.
Thank you for being my greatest inspiration.
I carry your heart in my heart always

Table of Contents

My Story 1

Introduction 5

What is Self-Love? 7

Step 1: **Discover Who You Are** (Self-Discovery) 13

Step 2: **Cultivate Self-Awareness** (Self-Awareness) 27

Step 3: **Fully Accept Yourself** (Self-Acceptance) 49

Step 4: **Practice Self-Compassion** (Self-Compassion) 65

Step 5: **Heal Your Past** (Self-Healing) 81

Step 6: **Know Your Worth** (Self-Worth) 101

Step 7: **Strengthen Your Confidence** (Self-Confidence) 117

Step 8: **Incorporate Self-Care** (Self-Care) 131

Step 9: **Keep Growing** (Self-Growth) 145

Step 10: **Love the World** (Self and Others) 161

Final Thoughts 175

References 177

Index 187

My Story

"Julia!" my father urgently spoke over my lifeless little body

The year is 1986. In a New Zealand hospital, the doctor and nurses desperately tried to resuscitate me after I was born not breathing. At the time of my birth, my lungs were filled with fluids which prevented me from taking my first breath. My face was already turning blue and the increasing seconds must have felt like an eternity for those around me. The medical staff anxiously attempted to revive my body with no success. Finally, my father gently blew air in my face, said my name again, and I took a deep inhalation. A sigh of relief filled the room or so I was told. This story has been recounted to me by my family for decades. Our breath is our lifeline and I don't think I took another deep breath for another thirty years but I digress. Let's start from the beginning…

My childhood was idyllic. I grew up quite sheltered and protected. I was raised in a loving and supportive household where I had all of my needs met. I was homeschooled up until the age of twelve. I also had a close group of friends and we all supported each other. I was the lead in a community play and I had dreams of becoming a famous actress one day. My parents taught me that I could do or be anything I wanted. As a young girl, I felt confident and believed in myself and my abilities, but all of that changed in the spring of 1998.

My mother found toxic mold growing out of the baseboards in our house which had been making us all sick, especially her. The plan was that my family and I would have the house professionally cleaned and return to our home in a few days. We never went back…

It turned out the mold was deadly and if we continued living in the house, we would either have serious health issues or face possible death. This was not the type of mold someone would find in their bathroom if they had not cleaned it. During the El Niño storms in California, there were heavy rains and flooding. However, since the contractors had not built our home properly, water had been seeping in behind the walls for years. Everything in my life changed forever.

I lost my home, my belongings, and my friends because we moved to a different city. As a result of our experience, my mom has had serious health issues ever since. We were involved in a litigious lawsuit for years. The stress of everything caused the breakdown of my parent's marriage. My father moved out and our relationship was never the same. Due to the circumstances, I started attending a charter school where I was picked on by my classmates for being different. For the first time in my life, I doubted myself, became self-critical and didn't feel good enough. During this period, I became introduced to my persistent inner critic who was always ready to rake me over the coals. I didn't feel pretty and I was going through that awkward stage of puberty you want to pass as quickly as possible. My hair was frizzy, my clothes were hand me downs since we lost our belongings, and I felt thin and gangly. I remember being taunted in the girl's locker room, finding trash in my backpack, the door being kicked in the bathroom stall while I was in it, but what hurt most of all was the feeling of being invisible. Most of the girls didn't seem to like me and I didn't feel included or welcome. To top it off, I also experienced my first and worst heartbreak in my life. I didn't feel equipped to handle all of the things thrown my way during that difficult time. I wanted to be someone else, anyone else, just not myself. So what did I do? I threw myself into being the best student I could be. I started getting straight A's and before I knew it, I was on the Honor Roll and then the Principal's List. I was at the top of my class. I figured I might not be well-liked, but at least I could be respected. Unfortunately, this began my addiction with perfectionism.

In order to feel worthy and deserving of love, I believed I needed to people-please and be perfect. To be honest, I'm not even sure what it means to be "perfect," except I thought it meant making everyone else happy and denying my authentic self. Since I hadn't healed the traumas of my past, they were showing up as patterns in my adult life. I lacked healthy boundaries and had a difficult time saying "no" to others. I never felt good enough. For a long time, I believed I needed to "do" or "be" something to prove my worthiness. My self-worth was tied up in my external achievements. I was extremely hard on myself and I didn't believe I deserved love. I struggled with my body image, career, and attracting the wrong men in my life.

With regards to dating and relationships, I gave my power away and lost my identity. Deep down, I felt inherently "unlovable" and feared abandonment if they saw the real *me*. I unconsciously attracted unhealthy relationships, one-sided friendships, and sought external validation. I lacked the self-love and self-compassion I needed to experience joy and fulfillment.

However, all of that changed during the pandemic. I finally had the time to make peace with my past and develop a healthy relationship with myself. I worked with a coach, read several self-help books, and did the inner healing work. I started being more vulnerable, showing up authentically, and embracing my true self. I released unhealthy attachments and the expectations of me, all the while remembering I was inherently enough. I began to recapture how I felt as a young girl:

confident, empowered, but most of all, *worthy*. After embarking on my own self-love journey two years ago, I learned that everything I needed was already inside of me and I didn't need to "prove" myself to be worthy and loved. I decided to turn my pain into purpose and since then I've made it my mission to help encourage and support others on their self-love journey's. I have coached women from across the globe in reclaiming the self-love that is their birthright. Today I incorporate what I have learned to help and support as many women as possible in achieving their goals and manifesting their dreams. I no longer feel like the victim of my story but rather the heroine who has taken control of her life. Do I still experience low self-worth days? Of course, but they are less common and don't get me down for long. Self-love is a daily practice, but once you have the foundation it makes life a whole lot easier. Loving yourself offers a deeper understanding of who you truly are and this knowledge will light the way of your path. This is the transformative power of self-love.

Introduction

"Love yourself first and everything else falls into line. You really have to love yourself to get anything done in this world" -Lucille Ball

Welcome! I am so excited you are here. As mentioned earlier, I am a self-love coach who helps women heal their relationships with themselves and create the life of their dreams. You might think to yourself why wouldn't an individual just go to therapy if they were struggling? What makes a coach any different? Coaching and therapy both have their strengths, but they are essentially different in nature. Both focus on the present, however therapy often focuses on the past while coaching generally focuses on the future. Coaching is a partnership that helps the client become clear on their goals, create a plan, and holds them accountable for following through. It tends to be an interactive process that is fun, fast-paced, and results-oriented. Breakthroughs and transformations are common. Limiting beliefs are replaced with realistic thoughts and it can be a powerful experience.

As a self-love coach, I have witnessed firsthand the incredible "aha moments" and transformations all made possible through the art of self-love. In essence, self-love is an art in that it is an expression of how we feel about ourselves. Self-love has the capacity to alter the very fiber of our being and show us opportunities we may have never believed were possible for us. In this book, I will outline the 10 steps I have discovered are essential for experiencing true self-love. Keep in mind that these 10 steps or pillars of self-love do not have to be in sequential order as every individual's self-love experience is as unique as a fingerprint. These steps are intended to serve as a guide and resource for anyone embarking on a self-love journey or seeking to improve their relationship with themselves.

I will also be sharing the wins and success stories of women just like you who were ready to make a change and improve their relationship with themselves. These individuals struggled with low self-worth, self-doubt, and limiting beliefs that were preventing them from achieving their goals. Once they did the healing work, they were able to start speaking kindly to themselves, practice self-compassion, and own their power in ways they never had before. These ladies achieved a greater sense of balance and purpose in their lives which allowed them to step into their higher callings. As well, these incredible women were able to attract new friendships, amazing relationships, exciting careers, traveling adventures, and fall in love with themselves and their bodies as a result of our work together:

"I cannot express what a long road it took me to be open and to finally have found Julia. Through my entire 47 years, through divorce, unhealthy friendships, isolation, unhealthy family relationships, unhealthy habits, etc., I finally feel like I actually matter. Julia has brought me peace in my mind and my life. Self-love is a long journey and without Julia's counsel, I would not be where I am today. Nothing can express my gratitude" -Sam (former client)

"I'm still blown away at the value that has been packed in our time together. It's like having a therapist, listening ear, and accountability partner all in one. I've done it all. Fifteen years of various modalities, including EMDR. Nothing-I mean nothing-has been as powerful as this self-love journey with Julia."
-Anna (former client)

What is Self-Love?

"To fall in love with yourself is the first secret to happiness"
-Robert Morley

Let's talk about self-love! There are a lot of misconceptions about self-love floating around out there, so we will begin by debunking ten common myths:

10 Self-Love Myths:

1. Self-Love is Egotistical or Selfish

Self-love is not a sense of entitlement or putting your needs above everyone else's. This myth implies that you believe you are better than others or that self-love is not in line with spirituality. The reality is that when you believe you are worthy and love yourself, you have more love to give others. We cannot give if we are feeling emptiness or lack. When we celebrate our strengths, it lifts others up. We cannot do it all alone. On the contrary, we tap into our greatest power when we connect with a Higher Power (ex. God or The Universe).

2. Self-Love is Vain or Superficial

There is a common misconception that self-love is all about one's looks or appearance. The myth here is that self-love is shallow, narcissistic, and self-involved. The truth is that loving yourself is recognizing your value does *not* lie in your physical appearance. To love yourself means caring about your physical, mental, spiritual, and emotional well-being. Self-love is practicing self-compassion and not feeling the need to be perfect. It is embracing the parts of yourself society has conditioned you to reject.

3. *Self-Love Prevents Self-Growth*

The idea that if you love yourself, it will hinder your self-development could not be more untrue! In fact, self-love encourages introspection and reflection which promotes self-growth. Self-love is a continual process of self-improvement and setting goals. You won't stop trying to better yourself or become lazy if you love yourself.

4. *Self-Love is Self-Care*

The two terms are often used interchangeably, however they are not the same. Self-care is an action or a way to show you love yourself. For example, getting a massage, cooking a meal for yourself, going on a nature walk, etc. Self-love is accepting and caring for yourself just as you are and recognizing your inherent worthiness.

5. *Self-Love is a Trend*

Self-love has been around forever. Well almost! The concept of self-love dates back to the Ancient Greeks and time of Buddha. It is not a millennial fad or Gen Z trend, but rather a way to feel secure in ourselves so that we have more to offer others.

6. *Self-Love is Being Happy All the Time*

Loving yourself is <u>not</u> toxic positivity. On the contrary, self-love is allowing yourself to experience all of your emotions with grace and compassion. We all struggle and have bad days, but the most important thing we can do when we are going through a difficult time is to practice self-compassion and love ourselves unconditionally.

7. *Self-Love is Only for People Struggling*

Self-love is for everyone regardless if you are struggling or not. In fact, self-love helps buffer negative emotions and reduces stress. Self-love can also be used preventatively to alleviate unnecessary struggling or suffering (ex. overthinking, self-criticism, etc.). Anyone can benefit from loving and showing themselves compassion.

8. *Self-Love is a Destination*

Self-love is a journey and a daily practice which connects you to your authentic self. It's not about being perfect, reaching some final place, or others' perceptions. Loving yourself is a constant commitment rather than somewhere you arrive. Self-love is never-ending and we are continually moving closer to our true nature. It is not a "one-size-fits-all" endeavor, but rather a deeply personal quest leading us to our higher selves.

9. *Self-Love Means You Don't Need Others*

Self-love is the foundation for all of our other relationships. In order to fully receive love, we must first love ourselves and in turn we will have more love to give others. Loving ourselves does not mean that we have to sacrifice our relationships. The reality is that self-love reminds us of our common humanity and inherent worthiness. Self-love is an excellent way to improve our relationships with others because we are able to clearly express what we want and need.

10. *Self-love isn't Essential*

This is a common misconception surrounding self-love which couldn't be further from the truth. Being kind and loving to ourselves is as essential as the air we breathe and the water we drink, because the love we have for ourselves extends to everyone else. We cannot give from an empty cup and it all starts with self-love.

Now that we've discussed what self-love isn't, we will explore what loving yourself actually means. This book will cover the 10 pillars of self-love and how to implement them into your life. Self-love is a state of mind in which you fully accept and value yourself. It means embracing all the parts of yourself, including what you have been conditioned by society to deny or change. Self-love is permitting yourself to make mistakes and releasing the need to be perfect. It is believing in yourself, feeling inherently worthy, and not allowing others to determine who you are. Unconditional self-love is your birthright and your true essence. When we show ourselves love and compassion and remember our common humanity, we find a greater sense of purpose and meaning in our lives.

Loving yourself is a constant act of being gentle and compassionate towards yourself and caring for your well-being. It is continually loving and holding space for yourself in those dark moments while tapping into the unconditional love within you. Self-love is something you do AND something you embody. It's a daily practice and commitment. It is more than a thing; it's a way of life. Loving yourself means living in alignment with your values and connecting to your higher self. It is listening to your intuition and inner wisdom. Self-love is a radiant energy you exude from the inside out while embracing who you truly are. It is an inner knowing that you are capable, worthy, and deserving of a beautiful life. Self-love is embracing your inner magic and not allowing anyone to dim your light. You are a phenomenal and extraordinary being with unlimited potential. You are one-of-a-kind and there has never been or will ever be another *you*. What's not to love? Let's conclude this section by taking a look at 5 amazing self-love benefits:

5 Self-Love Benefits:

1. Improves Mental and Physical Health

Studies have shown that positive self-talk helps reduce stress, anxiety, and depression. It can also strengthen physical and emotional health, improve sleep, and enhance overall well-being. Additionally, self-love can encourage healthier choices and increase emotional resilience. When we love ourselves, we are less likely to engage in self-sabotaging behaviors and more likely to make ourselves a priority.

2. Boosts Confidence and Motivation

Loving yourself can empower you to feel good in your skin and show up as the highest version of yourself. Self-love improves body image and confidence, thereby boosting attractiveness. When you love yourself, you exude a confident, powerful energy that is irresistible. Self-love can also increase productivity, passion, enthusiasm, and the ability to reach your full potential.

3. Increases Happiness and Life Satisfaction

When we fully accept and love ourselves, we are not as focused on other's opinions or seeking external validation. We generally do not take things as personally or allow our inner critic to run the show. We recognize self-doubt when it comes up and embrace our quirks and imperfections. Self-love encourages us to focus on our strengths and positive attributes. Accepting and loving ourselves grants us the right to take responsibility for our lives which can lead to genuine happiness.

4. *Improves Empathy and Relationships*

Self-love means offering ourselves kindness and compassion which ripples out into our other relationships. It increases our sense of empathy and understanding toward others. In order to attract the love we seek, we first need to value and respect ourselves. There is nothing more attractive than a person who is confident and loves themselves. Loving ourselves also encourages us to take our power back and to not be dependent on others for approval or validation. This provides an optimal environment for relationships to thrive. It can also reduce insecurities, jealousy, anger, and unhealthy patterns in relationships. Self-love is essential for effective communication and setting healthy boundaries with others. We teach others how to treat us. All of our relationships are based on a relationship with ourselves. Remember you are your longest relationship.

5. *Enhances Authenticity*

Loving yourself increases self-awareness, offers the space to be vulnerable, and fully express yourself. It also strengthens self-efficacy and the ability to trust yourself. Self-love can cause you to feel more capable and willing to get outside of your comfort zone. This not only contributes to your own well-being but also benefits those around you. Self-love can help you inspire and become a role model to others by encouraging them to shine their light too.

Step 1

Discover Who You Are
(Self-Discovery)

"Self-discovery begins with self-love. You have to love yourself enough to find yourself" -Nitin Namdeo

Who are you, *really*? The first pillar of self-love is to find out who you truly are. Self-love includes treating yourself as you would a friend, but before a friendship can be built, you must get to know the other person and learn about who they are. Self-discovery provides this incredible opportunity: acquainting yourself with the real you! This may include: your favorite things, what you love, who you love, what matters to you, but most importantly your inner essence. Once you know and understand yourself, you will have a better idea of where you are going and where you want to be. The journey of self-discovery is an exciting adventure which offers a sense of clarity and awareness of who you currently are and the potential within you. Discovering yourself can provide insight into your unique purpose which only you can fulfill in this world. Self-discovery also offers you a profound understanding of your identity, character, and true personality. Additionally, you will develop a deeper sense of your personal story and the experiences which shaped who you are today. The process of self-discovery is similar to peeling an onion, each layer removed brings you closer to the truth of who you are.

On this incredible journey, you will find out who you are when everything external is stripped away. It is so easy for our identity to be tied up in our family, friendships, relationships, appearance, career, finances, belongings, social status, etc. and we can lose sight of who we are underneath it all. This was one of my biggest struggles when my family and I lost everything-who was I when the things I had relied on disappeared? As the years passed, I had to do some soul-searching and figure out my purpose in life. Discovering your inner truth is an essential aspect of self-love. It also provides a solid foundation on which to stand when life throws the inevitable tests and challenges your way.

During the voyage of self-discovery, you will develop a greater sense of self-knowledge and the ability to understand your motives and life decisions. Knowing yourself on a deeper level will make you feel more confident and empowered. When we know ourselves, we are less likely to be influenced by the opinions of others because we stand firm in the truth of who we are. We do not allow society to dictate our worth or make us feel inferior. This clear sense of self provides the confidence and courage to stand up for ourselves and others. Discovering yourself will help you become grounded in your values and what matters most to you so that you can design your life accordingly.

Developing and cultivating the virtues within can also help connect you to your authenticity and inner truth on your self-discovery journey. In her inspiring book, *The Virtues Project: Simple Ways to Create a Culture of Character*, author Linda Kavelin Popov outlines the 52 virtues found throughout the major world religions and spiritual texts. In the Baha'i Writings, this concept is beautifully expressed: *"Regard man as a mine rich in gems of inestimable value. Education can, alone, cause it to reveal its treasures, and enable mankind to benefit there from."* Remember that you already have everything you need within you. Once you discover who you are and your purpose in this world, you can use your gifts and talents to serve humanity.

As you embark on this exciting search to discover the real you, you will rediscover your purpose and the events in your life which have contributed to your unique hero's journey. Throughout history, the Hero's Journey has been used as a model for the protagonist's adventure and subsequent victory. Influenced by acclaimed psychiatrist Dr. Carl's Jung's analytical psychology, author Joseph Campbell popularized the Hero's Journey (or monomyth) in modern culture. The protagonist encounters 17 stages which we will explore in this chapter. This template is used in popular films such as Star Wars, Harry Potter, Indiana Jones, The Wizard of Oz, and many Disney movies, including The Lion King, Moana, Finding Nemo, etc. The Hero's Journey is symbolic of the trials and tribulations we face in life and how we can overcome the obstacles placed in our path. An essential aspect of self-discovery is rewriting your story with yourself as the hero rather than the victim. You are the main character of your narrative and hold the pen in your hand. In Chapter 7, I will offer tips on how to harness your main character energy. It can be truly freeing and empowering to take control of your story and own the special role you were destined to play in your life.

The 17 Stages of the Hero's Journey:

Stage 1: *The Call to Adventure*

The hero's journey begins when the hero is called to abandon their mundane and normal life to go out into the great unknown. In this stage, the protagonist is asked to leave behind what is considered safe and familiar in search of something beyond their ordinary life. An opportunity has presented itself that the hero must further investigate (ex. going back to school, building a new business, creating a family, major life transitions, etc.).

Stage 2: *Refusal of the Call*

Obstacles such as insecurities, fears, duties, or responsibilities stand in the hero's way from embarking on their adventure. The protagonist is plagued with uncertainties and unforeseen challenges. The hero may question themselves or their ability to succeed in their endeavor and these hesitations may block them from initially moving forward (ex. self-doubt, limiting beliefs, past traumas, etc.).

Stage 3: *Supernatural Aid*

Once the hero has committed to their quest (consciously or unconsciously), their magical helper appears. Assistance arrives in the form of a mentor, guide, or earth angel who helps illuminate the path of the hero. This individual may gift their prodigy with a special artifact or talisman which will aid them later on in their adventure. The mentor provides the tools that the protagonist requires on their journey (ex. teacher, role model, divine intervention, inspirational book, etc.).

Stage 4: *Crossing the First Threshold*

During this stage, the hero leaves behind what is certain and established for the great unknown. Here the protagonist crosses into the field of adventure and embarks on their quest. The hero faces unknown fears and dangers where the rules and limits are undisclosed (ex. going on a first date after a painful breakup, taking a solo trip, signing up for a new class, prioritizing self-care, etc.).

Stage 5: *Belly of the Whale*

This step symbolizing the final release of the hero's former life. The protagonist encounters a difficult challenge or setback which marks the beginning of them shedding their old self for a new and transformed being. Originating from the Biblical story of Jonah who enters the belly of a whale and returns reborn, this analogy represents a complete metamorphosis. The hero will not be the same person they were who began their journey (ex. stress at work, discord at home, body image struggles, mental health issues, etc.).

Stage 6: *The Road of Trials*

Here the protagonist faces a series of trials on their journey. These ordeals serve as a catalyst for the hero's personal growth and discovering their true character. Also known as the figurative *"slaying of the dragon,"* these tests often appear in threes. Failure and setbacks are common, yet the hero is committed and will not let anything stand in their way. Barriers are crossed and glimpses of the victories to come are on the horizon (ex. experiencing a setback in recovery, reverting to old habits, self-sabotaging behavior, etc.).

Stage 7: *Meeting the Goddess*

After much change and upheaval, the meeting of the goddess signifies a place of respite for the hero after an arduous voyage. This stage is marked by the meeting of an advisor or trusted individual who need not be female, yet will provide the hero with guidance and wisdom. The goddess offers hope, reassurance, and unconditional love to the hero on their journey (ex. reuniting with an old friend, connecting with your community, etc.).

Stage 8: *Woman as the Temptress*

In this stage, the hero encounters desires, temptations, or distractions which make them consider abandoning their journey. Again this does not need to be a female, but someone or something who potentially stands in the way of the hero achieving their goals. This stage is symbolic of the temptations the hero may face, but is not necessarily indicative of any particular gender. The protagonist feels torn and must either overcome or avoid their temptations (ex. a toxic ex returns, triggers, insecurities resurface, etc.).

Stage 9: *Atonement with the Father/Abyss*

During this emotional stage, the hero confronts a part of themselves they have been trying to avoid. This step is represented by a powerful, father-like figure, yet it need not be male. This symbol signifies the all-encompassing force which has held power over the hero in their life. The protagonist discovers that they are actually the one in control and more capable than they had previously realized. The darkness and the light are finally reconciled (ex. facing a fear, healing a trigger, taking someone off the pedestal, believing in yourself and your abilities, etc.).

Stage 10: *Apotheosis*

In order for the hero to succeed, the old self must die so that a new being may emerge. During this stage, a great realization has occurred and the hero is confident and resolved to handle whatever is thrown their way. The protagonist has a new outlook and perception of themselves and the world. Breakthroughs and "aha moments" are prevalent and a deeper understanding and sense of clarity are made manifest (ex. releasing the past, ending a toxic relationship, setting healthy boundaries, etc.).

Stage 11: *The Ultimate Boon*

The hero has achieved the goal of their quest. All of the previous steps were intended to purify and cultivate the virtues within the main character. Good has triumphed over evil. This is the climax of the story where the protagonist has overcome their fears and the challenges they faced to receive their ultimate reward (ex. self-love, inner peace, personal freedom, healthy relationships, fulfilling career, happy home life, etc.).

Stage 12: *Refusal of the Return*

After the hero has experienced their transformation, it is now time to return to the ordinary world or everyday life, however the hero may initially not wish to do so. The protagonist may prefer to stay in their bubble of bliss and enlightenment, instead of going out into the world and sharing what they have learned with others (ex. potential relapses, avoidance behavior, denial, etc.).

Stage 13: *The Magic Flight*

This magical step is represented by a leap of faith taken by the hero. The protagonist isn't sure how they will continue their journey, yet they believe they will be guided and they are divinely assisted. The hero trusts that God/The Universe has their back and that everything will turn out for the best. In this stage, the hero's mission is greater than themselves which will no doubt lead them to succeed (ex. sharing your learnings, writing an inspiring book, starting a charity, creating a non-profit, etc.).

Stage 14: *Rescue from Without*

Even though the hero has achieved their goals, they may still need support in actualizing their mission. The protagonist will face a new struggle on their journey and will be rescued by some unexpected help or assistance. This stage is marked by a sense of common humanity and is a reminder that even a hero cannot do it all alone (ex. a mystery investor, family support, community assistance, etc.).

Stage 15: *Crossing the Return Threshold*

The hero officially returns back to the real world and shares their new-found insight and wisdom to serve others. The crossing of the return threshold is symbolic of a complete rebirth. In this stage, the protagonist must be willing to face old triggers and the harshness of the world, while not allowing it to steer them away from their vision. This step is marked by a return to normalcy and everyday life (ex. coming home from a trip, finishing a novel, graduating school, etc.).

Stage 16: *Master of the Two Worlds*

In this step, the hero has triumphantly mastered themselves and their life. Their outer world now reflects their inner world. The protagonist has discovered how strong, capable, and resilient they truly are. The lessons they learned and the personal growth they experienced cannot be taken away from the hero (ex. releasing control, letting go of attachments, ignoring your inner critic, etc.).

Stage 17: *Freedom to Live*

The traumas of the past have been healed and the fears of the future have vanished so that the hero may live in the present moment. In this stage, the protagonist realizes that they do not need to do or be anything because they were inherently enough all along. The hero has taken control of their life and experiences true freedom and liberation (ex. releasing other's opinions, owning your story, living your dreams, etc.).

As you can see, the Hero's Journey is a way to reinvent your story with a new hopeful perspective. You can reevaluate the stories you have told yourself about who you are and what is possible for you while examining if they still ring true for you. Remember it is never too late to rewrite the script of your life. As the hero of your story, you may reflect on your life thus far and reconsider the meaning of certain events which have transpired. Your unique adventure may contain multiple journey's and that is completely normal. We are multifaceted beings who can experience many lifetimes all in one lifespan.

Alchemy is another important aspect of any Hero's Journey, which is the magical process of transforming one thing to another. Much like a piece of coal can turn into a diamond, a caterpillar metamporhisizes into a butterfly, or the ugly duckling becomes a swan; the beauty was there all along. Alchemy can refer to physical materials such as turning metal into gold, but it can also represent a spiritual evolution. The protagonist of the story can transmute their past pain and suffering into meaning and purpose which is truly empowering. When you undergo a spiritual transformation, you are not the same person you were when you began the journey. You may look and sound the same, but you will have transitioned into a more conscious and enlightened version of yourself.

When I first began my self-love journey, many fears and doubts emerged. In reality, I was actually afraid of losing my old self in exchange for the new person I would become. When we release who we used to be and embrace who we truly are, it can make us question ourselves and our place in the world. The truth is: we have only evolved into another version of ourselves and have become better acquainted with the beautiful light that exists within. The journey of self-discovery will revolutionize your relationship with yourself in ways you never thought possible. As the hero of your story, you do not wait to be saved or rescued but instead create your own legend. Too often we look outside ourselves for magical power and forget that within us lies all the treasures of the universe and that we can write our own happily ever after. Now we will explore the power of self-discovery firsthand with my former client Anna's story:

Anna's Story

Anna is a beautiful, empathetic, and introspective young woman from an affluent family who has the world on a string. She is smart, talented, and capable; however, she didn't always see herself this way. When she came to me for help, she had been in and out of rehab several times, struggled with anxiety and depression, and experienced a low sense of self-worth. Anna suffered from shame, perfectionism, and a lack of purpose. She had undergone many traumas in her life and wanted to heal her wounds. Anna hoped to experience true self-love and forgiveness, yet she had difficulty knowing what she wanted and how to effectively express her needs. She had always been dependent on others, yet she longed to feel emotionally and financially independent. She aspired to travel the world and experience true freedom but her unhealthy patterns were getting in the way. Anna had "sugar daddies" and attracted unhealthy relationships.

As a little girl, she was praised on her appearance rather than the qualities and virtues she possessed. Her identity was tied in with her looks and this caused her feelings of inferiority and insecurity. The process of discovering her true self and releasing others' expectations of her was a truly freeing experience in her journey. Anna stopped viewing herself as dependent or a burden to her family. She developed a greater peace of mind and a renewed sense of confidence and empowerment surrounding her abilities. The last time we spoke, she had moved into her own place and was exploring her career options. She stopped manifesting toxic relationships with men and had begun a new friendship with a man who was kind and respectful. Anna is discovering her life's purpose and focusing on the abundance in her life. She is attracting her community of spiritual, like-minded individuals who possess similar goals. Anna is a free spirit, wild at heart, and marches to the beat of her own drum. She recently took a cross-country trip and is planning more traveling adventures in the future. Anna dreams of one day building her own nature-based, holistic health center which would serve those on their healing and recovery journey. She rewrote her life story and changed the ending with herself as the hero. Anna did the inner work and is now reaping the rewards.

Discovering who you are looks like:

- Taking a personality test (ex. Myers-Brigg, Enneagram, VIA Strengths, The Big 5, etc.)
- Making a list of your 5 core values
- Writing down your 10 favorite qualities or traits you possess
- Journaling on your major life events
- Contemplating your top gifts and talents and how you can use them to help others
- Making a list of things you are passionate about
- Keeping a diary or journal
- Reflecting on which virtues you exemplify and which you want to develop
- Trying something new
- Getting outside your comfort zone

Activity #1:

Your Hero's Journey

Instructions: Based on the 17 Stages of the Hero's Journey, write down one way you have experienced each stage in your life thus far (ex. major heartbreak, going back to school, life transition, body images struggles, addiction, etc.). How have these experiences brought out the hero in you?

Activity #2:

Discover your Archetype

An archetype is a persona which is represented across time and cultures. Dr. Carl Jung defines archetypes as: *"universal, primal symbols and images that derive from the collective unconscious."* Based off of Carl Jung's 12 Archetypes, take the quiz below to find out your archetype: https://archetypes.jilecek.cz

Activity #3:

Find your Ikigai

Ikigai is a Japanese term that translates into your *"reason for being."* Although the word originates back to the Heian period (794-1185), it became popularized by Japanese psychiatrist Dr. Mieko Kamiya in 1966. She described it as what gives our lives meaning and fulfillment. In this activity, you will discover your individual path or purpose based on the unique intersections of your life.

Instructions: Draw four concentric (overlapping) circles with a question in each one to answer:

1. What do you love to do?
2. What are you good at?
3. What can you get paid for?
4. What does the world need?

Observe where your answers overlap (center space). This will provide insight into your natural talents and the major themes in your life (see next page).

How to Find Ikigai

What you love

passion — mission

Your strengths — IKIGAI — The world needs

profession — vocation

What you can be paid for

Dr. Mieko Kamiya (1979)

Step 2

Cultivate Self-Awareness
(Self-Awareness)

"To know yourself, you must sacrifice the illusion that you already do" -Vironika Tugaleva

So far we have delve deeper into your inner essence and what makes you, *you*. In this exciting chapter, we will examine and analyze your predominant thoughts, feelings, and behaviors and how they have impacted your life thus far. Self-awareness is a state of consciousness where we observe ourselves and recognize our strengths and weaknesses. Keep in mind that a "weakness" is just an area of our lives which provides an opportunity for growth and improvement. Becoming self-aware also means having the ability to observe how we portray ourselves to the world and how we are perceived by others. Self-awareness includes understanding the meaning behind our emotions, examining our motives, and observing ourselves more objectively. To become self-aware also means recognizing how the past influences your perception of the present and questioning if what is familiar is continuing to serve you.

Self-awareness can be as simple as checking in with yourself and asking: *"What am I thinking? What am I feeling? What am I doing?"* So often we live our lives on auto-pilot and lack awareness of the present moment. Engaging in mindful activities such as nature walks, deep breathing, yoga, meditation, playing with pets or kids, etc. can help increase awareness of yourself and your surroundings. Practicing mindfulness is also an excellent tool to enhance your level of self-awareness and prioritize what is meaningful in your life. Be sure to set aside time each day for things that light you up from the inside out and bring you joy.

Acquiring self-awareness is a critical step on the self-love journey to ensure that we are living in alignment with our authentic self. We will investigate reoccurring themes, life patterns, unhealthy habits, and persistent struggles which may have held you back from moving forward. For example, I used to attract emotionally unavailable men, one-sided friendships, and unfulfilling jobs into my life without knowing why. Once I became self-aware of the energy I was projecting out into the world, I stopped manifesting these situations. There is no such thing as a "coincidence," when it refers to similar events that keep recurring over and over again in our lives. It is essential to take notice and cultivating self-awareness is key.

"You see what you expect to see, Severus."

Any Harry Potter fans out there? This line from *Harry Potter and the Deathly Hallows* suggests that one's perception shapes their reality. Interestingly enough, Professor Dumbledore may have been on to something that neuroscience is currently in the process of uncovering. It turns out that our minds unconsciously alter our perception of reality to fit our expectations. Trippy right? Our past experiences even influence how we see certain things and situations. The brain is constantly looking for shortcuts and making inferences about what is happening around us.

In this chapter, you will develop a deeper awareness and understanding of the inner workings of your mind. This information can provide insight into how you perceive your world and how to challenge the assumptions which are no longer benefitting you. We will also look at the role of the inner critic in fostering self-doubt as well as recognizing unhelpful cognitive biases and cognitive distortions which may be holding you back. Next, we will explore the 4 Self-Awareness Archetypes along with simple ways to help increase your level of self-awareness. We will also delve deep into Emotional Intelligence, Dr. Carl Jung's 4 Theories of Consciousness, shadow work, and developing greater awareness into the hidden parts of yourself. Finally, we will discuss how to more effectively get out of your comfort zone and become more conscious in your everyday life.

Did you know that over 90% of your thoughts are *unconscious*? You may not even realize the extent of how much your thoughts are influencing your actions and behavior. Studies show that people greatly overestimate their level of self-awareness. If you want to master your life, you must first become aware of your thoughts. This section will provide psychological tips and tools to bring the unconscious into your conscious awareness. Self-awareness includes silencing our inner critic and releasing self-judgement. Your inner critic is that negative voice inside your head which loves to highlight your greatest insecurities, find fault with you, and refuse to let you off the hook. The inner critic makes you feel small, insignificant, and unworthy. It can sound like, *"You're not pretty enough," "You can't do it," "You look fat," "There's something wrong with you,"* etc. Totally harsh, right? Unfortunately, we all have this little pessimistic voice within us, however whether we choose to listen and identify with it is a whole other story. The inner critic only has power if we allow it to take over and believe the lies it spews. Let's consider a real-life example of the inner critic from one of my former clients:

Sam's Story Part 1

Sam is an attractive, funny, and successful woman who had one of the worst inner critics I've ever encountered. *"My mind is my enemy,"* was literally something she wrote on her client in-take form before we started working together! Sam's problem was that she identified with her negative thoughts and believed them to be facts. The truth was that her inner critic was not her own, but the voices of her parents and the patriarchal society in which she was brought up. Sam explained that her parents had wanted a boy instead of a girl, which had caused her to never feel good enough. These unhealthy and limiting beliefs had been passed down for generations.

When Sam came to me, she told me that she didn't know who she truly was. Her early childhood consisted of making others happy, which had led to her own interests and passions remaining on the back burner. Sam also found herself using distractions to avoid spending time with herself. This led to a sense of alienation and disconnection from her true being. Sam was afraid to face her past and heal the traumas which had haunted her growing up. As she so aptly stated, *"I was protecting myself from myself."* Since this and many other wounds were not healed, she struggled with self-doubt, people-pleasing, and low self-worth. Sam often put herself down in the hopes of making others feel more comfortable and she didn't value herself. This was affecting her career, relationships, and sense of purpose. In both her relationships and career, she lacked healthy boundaries and didn't stand up for herself.

One of her greatest breakthroughs occurred when she stopped distracting and running away from herself to experience what she was truly feeling. Sam remarked that this was the first time she had sat with her uncomfortable and painful emotions and gave them the space to be. Doing this work takes courage, strength, and resilience all of which Sam's character so perfectly illustrates. She had stumbled upon the curious paradox, which is that the more we avoid something, the more we need to face it. Keep in mind that I am by no means saying that we should push ourselves before we are ready. Healing often comes in waves and I've found that it is often best to take a gentle and baby step approach. Sam's story is unique in that she was experiencing rapid results within 3 weeks into the program.

During our time together, Sam learned not to believe everything she thought and to challenge her limiting beliefs. She began questioning negative thoughts such as, *"I'm stupid,"* and asking herself where is this thought coming from and what is it trying to tell me. The self-critical thoughts which plagued her for as long as she could remember, loosened their hold and she finally felt, *"free and liberated."* Today she feels more than enough, that she deserves to take up space, and has stopped the cycle of self-doubt. Sam's story demonstrates that healing is indeed possible and now her mind is her greatest ally.

Upon completing the program, the fears which had been holding her back have been released. Currently, she is discovering her passions which include: social justice, diversity, and inclusion. Sam plans to spread the love in her community and engage in volunteer and service projects. She has also signed up for new classes and recently took up yoga. During one memorable yoga session, Sam had a powerful vision of hugging and comforting her 7 year-old-self which has made a profound impact on her healing journey. Sam now makes time for self-care without the usual guilt weighing her down. For the first time, she is enjoying her alone time and solitude. She was astonished by how much the program helped her and the positive changes she has witnessed. In our final session together Sam said, *"Today I am a different person who is excited about my life. I feel like the world is my oyster. The options feel endless, as if I can do anything."* I couldn't put it better myself!

What a brilliant testament to the process of silencing your inner critic and taking your power back! Here is my rule of thumb: if a thought makes you feel bad, it is probably not the truth. Our inner wisdom is kind, loving, and offers positive and constructive ways to improve ourselves free from shame or judgement. Obviously, shaming and blaming ourselves for our mistakes is detrimental to self-love, yet showing ourselves kindness and compassion is as necessary as the air we breathe. Becoming more aware of your thoughts and how they make you feel provides the opportunity to challenge your inner critic and reject the nonsense it is speaking to you. Instead, replace your self-defeating thoughts with a more truthful and realistic belief. For example, next time you make a mistake, consider what a friend would say to you and respond in a similar way. Try saying, *"I'm only human and we all make mistakes"* and forgive yourself without judgement. How we speak to ourselves determines the course of our lives.

Building a heightened awareness of our inner dialogue is a pivotal part of the self-love journey. Identifying and understanding cognitive biases and cognitive distortions can help shed light on our hardwired unconscious thinking patterns and how we can create new neural pathways in the brain. First, let's take a look at cognitive biases and how they alter our perceptions of the world around us. Cognitive biases cause us to be more inclined to favor or be against something which clouds us from a neutral outlook. Our brain utilizes these biases to help us filter vast amounts of complex information more quickly, however this can cause us to incorrectly misinterpret what is actually happening and make us less effective in our lives. There are over 180 types of cognitive biases, yet for the purposes of this book, we will examine 25 common cognitive biases:

25 Cognitive Biases:

1. *Blind Spot Bias*-failure to acknowledge our biases is a bias in itself (ex. believing you always see the world objectively).
2. *Confirmation Bias*-the search for proof that matches our existing beliefs and ignoring facts that contradict our opinion (ex. thinking you will always struggle financially because you have in the past).
3. *Backfire Effect*-when our core beliefs are challenged, it can cause us to believe them even more (ex. *"I don't care what she says, I'll never be beautiful"*).
4. *Anchoring Bias*-the first piece of information you receive influences everything you judge afterward (ex. whoever makes the first offer in a salary negotiation has the upper hand because they establish the standard).
5. *Availability bias*-the tendency to go with what first comes to mind (ex. accepting a limiting belief without questioning it first).
6. *Declinism*-we remember the past as better than it was and perceive the future as worse than it will likely be (ex. romanticizing the past and believing your best days are behind you).
7. *Pessimism Bias*-we overestimate the probability of negative outcomes (ex. *"I'll probably make a fool of myself during the speech"*).
8. *The Negative Feedback Instinct*-the tendency to spot flaws first (ex. noticing your imperfections rather than your strengths).
9. *Spotlight Effect*-we typically over-exaggerate how much people notice us (ex. most people are more consumed with themselves and less worried about what you are doing).

10. *Sunk Cost Fallacy*-the tendency to continue what we are doing because we have invested time, money, or energy into it (ex. staying in an unfulfilling relationship).
11. *Clustering Illusion*-finding meaning and significance which do not exist in random patterns (ex. *"I keep seeing the numbers 11:11. It's a sign I should get back together with my ex"*).
12. *Stereotyping*-assuming all individuals of a group are the same based on limited information (ex. *"all men cheat"*).
13. *Status Quo Bias*-we tend to prefer things to stay the same even if they do not serve us (ex. staying in a dead-end job instead of facing uncertainty).
14. *Hindsight Bias*-our inclination to perceive past events as more predictable than they are (ex. *"I should have known better"*).
15. *Shiny Object Syndrome*-our tendency to pursue something new instead of sticking with our original goals (ex. diet fads, "miracle" treatments, etc.).
16. *Instant Gratification*-choosing an immediate benefit over a more rewarding future return (ex. laying on the couch all weekend rather than moving your body).
17. *Moral Licensing*-convincing ourselves that a positive action will make up for poor behavior (ex. *"since I didn't get enough sleep, I will exercise in the morning"*).
18. *Ben Franklin Effect*-we tend to like those who we do favors for (ex. asking someone you want to connect with for help or support).
19. *Another Choice Myth*-the inclination to choose an alternative we know little about instead of dealing with the problem at hand (ex. avoiding an issue by moving to a new city).
20. *Choice-Supportive Bias*-we tend to exaggerate the benefits of an option after we choose it (ex. *"even though this car is compact, it gets excellent gas-mileage"*).

21. *Authority Bias*-we are more likely to be influenced and trust those in power (ex. politicians, celebrities, influencers, etc.).
22. *Suggestibility*-we are more vulnerable to suggestion than we may realize (ex. ads, the media, other's opinions, etc.)
23. *Third Person Effect*-we believe that others are more naïve and suggestible than we are (ex. perceiving other people as being more influenced by the media than ourselves).
24. *Ostrich Effect*-when things are difficult, we are more likely to bury our head in the sand and ignore negative information (ex. avoidance, procrastination, etc.).
25. *Selective Perception*-allowing our past experiences to influence how we perceive the world (ex. believing we are correct and others are wrong).

Now we will explore the influence cognitive distortions have on our self-talk. Introduced by American psychiatrist Dr. Aaron Beck in the 1960's, cognitive distortions are thinking errors that lead to unhealthy thoughts about ourselves and our environment. When our thoughts are irrational, exaggerated, or inaccurate, it can lead to unhelpful thinking patterns which influence our emotions and behavior. Cognitive distortions keep us stuck in negative thinking traps, convincing ourselves that these false thoughts are true. This inner dialogue can turn into self-critical beliefs which hold us back from reaching our full potential. Becoming aware of our distorted thinking and challenging our thoughts can help improve our mental and physical health and the quality of our relationships. Countering and replacing a negative thought with a positive statement is an excellent way to address cognitive distortions. These are the 20 most common cognitive distortions:

20 Cognitive Distortions:

1. *Catastrophizing*-assuming the worst case scenario in a situation (ex. *"my boyfriend hasn't called me back so he probably got into a car accident"*).
2. *Mental Filtering*-observing through a limited point of view without seeing the bigger picture (ex. receiving 9 compliments and 1 criticism but focusing on the critical remark).
3. *Polarized Thinking*-engaging in *"all or nothing"* or *"black or white"* thinking and not seeing the gray area (ex. *"I didn't get the job so I'm a failure"*).
4. *Magnification*-exaggerating the importance of an event (ex. *"everyone saw me slip up and now they won't like me"*).
5. *Minimization*-downplaying the significance of a situation (ex. *"it was nothing. Anyone could do it"*).
6. *Overgeneralization*-thinking all experiences or people are the same based on limited experience (ex. *"my ex was a jerk so there are no good guys out there"*).
7. *Jumping to Conclusions*-arriving at a verdict with little or no evidence (ex. *"my friend seemed irritated so I must have done something to upset her"*).
8. *Mind Reading*-presuming what another person is thinking or feeling (ex. *"he's awfully quiet so he probably doesn't like me anymore"*).
9. *Fortune Telling*-making a predication with little or no supportive evidence (ex. *"I'm starting to feel anxious so I'm going to pass out"*).
10. *Magical Thinking*-believing that certain actions will influence unrelated outcomes (ex. *"I'm a good person so bad things shouldn't happen to me"*).

11. *Blaming*-holding someone or something responsible for a negative event without looking at our possible role (ex. *"it is my parent's fault that I have these limiting beliefs"*).
12. *Personalization*-thinking we are to blame for events outside of our control (ex. *"I was a difficult child which caused my parents' divorce"*).
13. *Labelling*-assigning a judgement to oneself or someone else without all of the information (ex. *"I can't believe I said that. I'm so stupid"*).
14. *Always Being Right*-internalizing our thoughts and opinions as facts; feeling that being wrong is unacceptable (ex. *"I don't agree with her so she must be wrong"*).
15. *Should/Ought/Must Statements*-believing that things need to be a certain way; placing unrealistic standards on ourselves and others (ex. *"I should be married by now"*).
16. *Emotional Reasoning*-speculating that if we feel something, it is the objective truth (ex. *"I'm feeling lonely so I must be unlovable"*).
17. *Control Fallacies*-thinking that everything that happens to us is either all our fault or not our fault at all (ex. *"I was raised in a dysfunctional household which is why I attract toxic relationships"*).
18. *Fallacy of Change*-believing that others need to change to suit our needs (ex. trying to change a partner to fit your ideals).
19. *Fallacy of Fairness*-holding all situations to a standard of fairness or equity (ex. *"we're the same age so it's not fair that she found someone and I haven't yet"*).
20. *Heaven's Reward Fallacy*-thinking that if we lived in a fair world, we would be fairly rewarded for our efforts (ex. *"I work harder than she does and I should have gotten that promotion"*).

Where do you fall on the self-awareness scale? According to Harvard researcher, New York Times best-selling author, and organizational psychologist Dr. Tasha Eurich, there are 4 Self-Awareness Archetypes which demonstrate our level of self-awareness. Interestingly enough, research has shown that while most people believe they are self-aware, only 10-15 percent actually are. First, we will begin by examining the two primary types of self-awareness which are internal and external. Internal self-awareness refers to our ability to accurately perceive ourselves and our thoughts, feelings, and behaviors. On the other hand, external self-awareness deals with our ability to understand how others view us. For the purpose of this section, we will mainly focus on how we see ourselves, however it can be helpful to consider how others perceive us which can benefit our relationships and work environment. Let's take a look at the 4 Self-Awareness Archetypes, along with tips to improve our self-awareness:

The 4 Self-Awareness Archetypes:

1. <u>Seekers</u> -*(low internal self-awareness; low external self-awareness)*

They do not yet understand who they are or how they are perceived by others which may leave them feeling stuck and unfulfilled (tip: begin by taking your own self-discovery journey).

2. <u>Pleasers</u>-*(low internal self-awareness; high external self-awareness)*

They are overly concerned with how others view them and may overlook what is important to them (tip: focus your energy on what gives you joy).

3. <u>Introspectors</u>-*(low external self-awareness; high internal self-awareness)*

They are clear on who they are, but they are unaware of how others view them. These individuals do not challenge their own views, search for their blind spots, or ask for feedback which can harm their relationships and limit their success (tip: be open to feedback from trusted individuals and keep an open-mind).

4. Awares-*(high internal self-awareness; high external self-awareness)*

They know and understand who they are while also valuing the opinions of others (tip: continue to be on the lookout for potential blind spots).

4 Self-Awareness Archetypes

	Low External Self-Awareness	High External Self-Awareness
High Internal Self-Awareness	**Introspectors** — They know who they are but don't ask for feedback or explore their blind spots	**Awares** — They know who they are and they value feedback
Low Internal Self-Awareness	**Seekers** — They don't know who they are or how they are perceived by others	**Pleasers** — They are overly focused on how others view them

Dr. Tasha Eurich (2019)

Although psychoanalysts Dr. Carl Jung and Dr. Sigmund Freud did a great deal of research into the area of emotional intelligence, psychologist Dr. Daniel Goleman popularized the term in his #1 New York Times book, *Emotional Intelligence*. Emotional intelligence refers to the ability to observe, understand, and manage our emotions. Identifying and recognizing what we are feeling in any given moment is a self-love superpower. Cultivating self-awareness has many benefits including strengthening emotional intelligence, improving decision making, helping manage emotions and difficult situations, and boosting the likelihood of success. When you are self-aware, you have a deeper understanding of your wants and needs which can also improve your relationships.

Self-awareness also includes observing and understanding the dark and hidden aspects of ourselves in order to bring them into the light. In the classic book, *The Archetype and the Collective Unconscious*, Dr. Carl Jung outlines the 4 Theories of Consciousness: the persona, the anima/animus, the shadow, and the self. The persona, anima/animus, and the shadow are unconscious and the self is conscious. True self-awareness involves the integration of all levels of consciousness. The persona is the conformist version of ourselves that we show the world in order to be accepted and receive approval from others. This includes the masks we wear in various social situations. For example, a salesperson acts confident and self-assured, a caregiver behaves kindly and compassionately, a police officer exhibits strength and courage, etc. The anima (feminine) and animus (masculine) are the opposite gender qualities within us that have been repressed. For women, the animus symbolizes stereotypically male attributes such as assertiveness, analytical thought, decisiveness, etc. In men, the anima is represented by feminine qualities such as empathy, inspiration, intuition, sensitivity, and receptivity. For instance, a little girl is told she is "bossy" for behaving the same way as her male counterpart so she unconsciously represses this aspect of herself. The shadow represents the "dark" parts of ourselves we have suppressed and denied since childhood in order to be accepted and loved. It includes the thoughts, beliefs, and behaviors deemed unacceptable by those whose approval we sought the most. Finally, the self is the uniting of the unconscious and conscious into being. It is the integration of the mental disconnect of who we show the world versus who we truly are which leads to true self-awareness.

A notable aspect of shadow work is understanding our inner child wounds, core negative beliefs, and insecurities. In my course and coaching program, there is a module on shadow work since examining the hidden aspects of the psyche is an essential part of self-love. Shadow work offers a deeper understanding of our "darker" emotions such as fear, anger, shame, sadness, resentment, jealousy, etc. which we consider in order to heal trauma, unblock stuck energy, and acknowledge repressed emotions. This type of work helps identify our blind spots and bring these hidden aspects into our conscious awareness. It is essential to practice a non-judgmental attitude toward yourself when you are exploring your shadows. One of the biggest challenges of shadow work is that if you discover something you do not like about yourself, it is human nature to defend your beliefs as an act of self-preservation. For example, I used to fear that I wasn't good enough, which would cause me to people-please and overcompensate in order to conceal my self-doubt and insecurities. The real growth occurred when I was able to take responsibility for my actions and make a positive change. Taking accountability for our lives is truly freeing and empowering. Self-awareness means living in alignment with your core values and not allowing the beliefs or opinions of others to influence your decisions. For more support, feel free to check out my *Radical Self-Love Workbook* which includes shadow work, inner child healing, and releasing limiting beliefs activities on Amazon.com.

Comfort Zone vs. Growth Zone

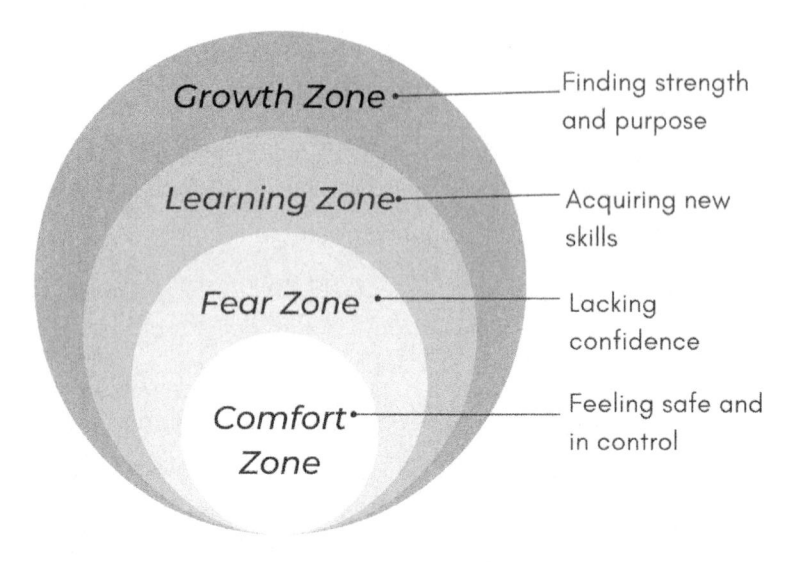

- **Growth Zone** — Finding strength and purpose
- **Learning Zone** — Acquiring new skills
- **Fear Zone** — Lacking confidence
- **Comfort Zone** — Feeling safe and in control

Tom Senninger (2000)

To conclude this section, we will examine how self-awareness provides the opportunity to assess the areas of your life where you may be *"playing it safe"* and how to expand outside your comfort zone and develop greater self-awareness. Leaving your comfort zone is a 4-step process resulting in reaching the growth zone. We start in our comfort zone where we feel safe, in control, and there is low risk. Next, we approach the fear zone in which we lack confidence, may make excuses, and begin to challenge ourselves. Afterward, we go to the learning zone where we acquire new skills and feel more competent. Here we are searching for new opportunities and challenges. Finally, we reach the growth zone where we set and achieve our goals, find our purpose, and live our dreams. Keep in mind that this process is not always linear and encountering setbacks or difficulties is normal.

Let's look at a real-life example: we begin with a novice surfer who is relaxing on a sandy beach (comfort zone). Now the surfer goes out into the ocean and gets wiped out by the waves (fear zone). Next, the surfer is practicing new moves and is feeling more confident in her abilities (learning zone). Finally, the surfer has entered a competition and is pursuing her aspirations (growth zone). The benefits of moving beyond your comfort zone include: developing a growth mindset, increased resilience, experiencing self-actualization, and self-efficacy. Self-actualization allows us to reach our full potential and self-efficacy is the belief that we are capable. Both terms will be reviewed in-depth in the following chapters. Here are 10 ideas to help you get outside of your comfort zone and enhance your level of self-awareness:

10 Self-Awareness Ideas:

1. Try a new hobby
2. Get creative (art, music, dance, etc.)
3. Go somewhere you've never been
4. Learn something new
5. Mix up your routine
6. Challenge your beliefs
7. Connect with new people
8. Protect your time and energy
9. Open up and be vulnerable with others
10. Release the need to be in control

Sofia's Story Part 1

"I get jealous sometimes and I don't know why. There's no reason for me to be, my boyfriend is wonderful and loves me but I still feel insecure and unsure of our

relationship at times," my client Sofia revealed one day during a session together. Sofia is a gorgeous, educated, and likable young woman, however she was struggling in her current relationship. This was a reoccurring theme in Sofia's relationship with her boyfriend, Tom. Tom would say or do something, Sofia would get triggered, and conflict would ensue. She would become suspicious and paranoid, fearing he would abandon her. Eventually, they would reconcile, yet sometimes their arguments would result in Sofia threatening to leave the relationship. She confided in me that she occasionally wished the union would dissolve so that she could avoid the uncomfortable emotions that she was feeling. I knew that she loved Tom and didn't actually want the relationship to end, however unhealed trauma in her childhood was rearing its ugly head in her adult relationship.

The triggers that Sofia experienced were the result of her own parents' unhealthy relationship and their subsequent divorce. The disillusion of Sofia's parents' marriage caused her mother to fall into a depression which prompted her to quickly jump into another relationship. Sofia's mother feared being alone and was drawn to codependent relationships. Observing her mother's experiences with love concerned Sofia, since she didn't want to end up in the same predicament. Sofia had trust and abandonment issues that had been passed down from her mother. These were unconscious fears without basis and there was no cause for them in her current relationship, yet they continued to plague her. Becoming aware of her triggers and healing her core wounds so that they would no longer surface in her life was pivotal. Self-awareness was key to her self-love journey. The last time we spoke, she was better able to identify and navigate her triggers as they showed up. Sofia chose not to run away, faced her fears, and is still with her boyfriend, Tom. Her willingness to bring her shadows into the light and heal herself are a testament to the strength of her character and her ability to experience true self-love. Sofia now feels more confident and secure in her relationship. She broke the cycle which will no doubt benefit future generations as well.

Cultivating self-awareness looks like:

- Monitoring your self-talk
- Questioning automatic thoughts
- Allowing yourself to feel your feelings
- Identifying and listing your triggers
- Releasing judgement of yourself and others
- Recognizing your primary coping mechanisms
- Identifying healthy alternative strategies
- Writing down your strengths and weaknesses
- Completing a body scan
- Asking for feedback

Activity #1:

Explore the Cave

Writer Joseph Campbell once said, *"The cave you fear to enter holds the treasure you seek."* Write down something you have been afraid to face about yourself. Where does this fear originate? How has this fear held you back from fully living your life? What can you do to acknowledge and heal this part of yourself?

Activity #2:

Cognitive Distortions

Instructions: For each of the following 20 thinking errors, write down an example from your own life. Next, counter the unhealthy belief with a more realistic thought:

1. Catastrophizing
2. Mental Filtering
3. Polarized Thinking
4. Magnification
5. Minimization
6. Overgeneralization
7. Jumping to Conclusions
8. Mind Reading
9. Fortune Telling
10. Magical Thinking
11. Blaming
12. Personalization
13. Labelling
14. Always Being Right
15. Should/Ought/Must Statements
16. Emotional Reasoning
17. Control Fallacies
18. Fallacy of Change
19. Fallacy of Fairness
20. Heaven's Reward Fallacy

Activity #3:

Self-Awareness Trifecta

Instructions: Answer the following questions based on the 3 self-awareness categories:

Thoughts:

How do you explain and think about what happens to you? How do you speak to yourself? What thoughts typically arise during your day?

Emotions:

How well do you understand your thoughts and emotions? Do you react impulsively or try to observe and consider what you are feeling? Are you aware of why specific emotions come up?

Behaviors:

What types of events trigger you? Are you aware of why you react to certain situations in the same way? How do you act when things don't go your way?

Step 3

Fully Accept Yourself
(Self-Acceptance)

"The most terrifying thing is to accept yourself completely"
-Dr. Carl Jung

Do you accept yourself as you are in this moment or is there always something that you are unsatisfied with and want to change? Self-acceptance is the embracing of *all* the parts of ourselves, even the aspects we label as "flaws" or "imperfections." Self-acceptance means seeing and loving the entirety of who you are without exceptions or conditions. For example, *"I will love myself when I lose 25 lbs."* or *"I will love myself if I find my dream partner"* or *"I will love myself when I'm no longer depressed,"* etc. The practice of self-acceptance includes honoring the truth of who you were and who you currently are today. We cannot alter the past, but we can adjust course moving forward. Accepting yourself can be extremely difficult, especially if you are anything like how I used to be where when I made mistake, I would berate myself and feel like a failure. At a certain point, I recognized that my self-critical thoughts and beliefs were hindering my ability to achieve real progress and growth. If I wanted to make a change, I needed to show up more authentically and vulnerably in my life. It is so easy to hide behind the mask of perfectionism in order to receive approval and validation all the while forgetting whose acceptance counts the most: our own. Remember perfection does *not* exist, no matter how much society or social media will try to convince you.

Learning to fully accept ourselves means releasing the need to live up to unrealistic societal expectations and to people-please. Before I embarked on my own self-love journey, I struggled with wanting to make everyone else happy at the expense of my own needs. I would say "yes" when inside my heart was screaming "no," because I was under the false assumption that being a "good" person meant putting other's needs before my own. My worth became dependent on people's value judgements of me and not my inherent self. During this process, I lost a few friends, yet I found myself along the way and I began attracting healthier and more reciprocal relationships.

Being accepted and liked is a basic human instinct which we use in order to survive, but if it costs you your truth or authenticity, it is too high a price to pay. Instead of trying to conform or fit in with societal norms, embrace your quirks and what makes you unique. Ironically, once we learn to accept and love ourselves, others are more likely to as well and we are better able to accept others as they are. Accepting ourselves and feeling comfortable in our skin is such an attractive quality! It is also important to be aware of who you give your time and energy to and how you feel once they leave your presence. If you feel light and rejuvenated, this is a good energetic match, however if you feel a sense of heaviness or depletion, it might be time to reconsider the relationship. An excellent way to foster self-acceptance is to connect with individuals who are supportive and non-judgmental. Your support system should include people who *already* accept and believe in you.

In this chapter, we will explore ideas to develop greater self-acceptance, the power of radical self-acceptance, and ways to validate yourself. We will also consider the role of releasing self-abandonment and self-judgement, while cultivating self-patience in our ability to fully accept ourselves. Additionally, we will analyze the work of acclaimed psychologist Dr. Carl Rogers and his 3 Parts of the Self-Concept and the 7 Characteristics of a Fully Functioning Person as they relate to self-acceptance. Finally, we will distinguish the difference between body acceptance and body positivity along with tips to more fully accept and embrace your body. Let me be clear, self-acceptance does not mean that we cease to improve ourselves and set new goals. On the contrary, self-acceptance is the breeding ground for substantial and sustainable growth. Once we fully accept and affirm ourselves, we are able to make our dreams come true. Self-acceptance is a conduit for miracles.

Self-acceptance has so many benefits including: weakening negative self-talk, reducing the risk of anxiety and depression, improving emotional well-being, strengthening confidence, and increasing our ability for change. We are also better able to handle criticism and maintain our sense of who we are. When we do not accept ourselves, it is much easier to take things personally and doubt ourselves when faced with critical remarks. The ability to separate ourselves from other people's opinions is a true marker of self-acceptance. Accepting ourselves means releasing the thought that there is anything "wrong" with us or the incessant need to change or fix ourselves. As we will discuss later on in the chapter, this can be challenging in a society that profits off of our insecurities, however this is a monumental step in the self-love journey. If you are struggling with self-acceptance, here are 15 ways to more deeply and fully accept yourself:

15 Self-Acceptance Tips:

1. Remember you are a work in progress
2. Remind yourself that perfection doesn't exist
3. Stop questioning where you are in life
4. Release the need to judge yourself or others
5. Accept your flaws or weaknesses
6. Don't compare yourself to a past version of you
7. Quit the self-blame game
8. Stop identifying with your thoughts
9. Accept uncomfortable emotions
10. Allow yourself to grieve and release the past
11. Address and heal past trauma
12. Confront your fears
13. Embrace your body as it is
14. Enjoy your own company
15. Trust that everything will be okay

According to Dr. Tara Brach, author of *Radical Acceptance: Embracing Your Life with the Heart of a Buddha*, radical self-acceptance is the conscious effort and willingness to experience ourselves, our thoughts and feelings, and the realities of our lives. The idea of radical acceptance originated from Buddhist teachings which emphasize mindfulness and the ability to sit with our thoughts and emotions without resistance, but rather acceptance. When we are struggling or suffering, it is completely normal to want to repress, avoid, or reject our pain, however the practice of accepting whatever comes up can help ease our suffering and allow us to move through discomfort more quickly. Accepting ourselves has the potential to transform our reality and our relationship with ourselves.

Have you ever abandoned yourself? Self-abandonment means ignoring ourselves, our emotions, or our needs in order to gain approval or validation from others. It is putting other's opinions before ourselves and our well-being. Basically, self-abandonment is the antithesis of self-love because it is in essence rejecting yourself. Forsaking ourselves can lead to anxiety, depression, low self-esteem, and unhealthy relationships. It is impossible to build a healthy relationship with ourselves or others if we are constantly diminishing or discounting our own thoughts and feelings. Self-abandonment is a behavior often originating from family dynamics learned in childhood as something we observed or experienced. Abandoning ourselves includes not trusting our instincts, hiding aspects of ourselves, and refusing to honor our needs. It can also indicate that we believe others know more than we do and deferring to their judgement. Being overly critical of ourselves and displaying perfectionist or people-pleasing tendencies are examples of self-abandonment. When we accept and validate who we are, we can release the decision to abandon ourselves. Here are 15 ways to halt the destructive cycle of self-abandonment:

15 Tips to Stop Self-Abandonment:

1. Act in your own best interest
2. Trust yourself and your feelings
3. Stop second-guessing yourself
4. Show up authentically
5. Be honest and genuine
6. Acknowledge your wants and needs
7. Learn to say "no"
8. Practice assertive communication
9. Express your thoughts and feelings
10. Act in accordance with your values
11. Speak up for yourself

12. Maintain your autonomy in relationships
13. Define your non-negotiables
14. Address your emotional needs
15. Commit to your well-being

Now let's consider the role of self-judgement in the journey to self-acceptance. Self-judgement refers to the process of finding fault and criticizing ourselves. It begins with negative self-talk and turns into a judgmental and condemning viewpoint of who we are which makes self-acceptance nearly impossible. This may include comparing, labeling, or beating ourselves up. Perfectionists beware! Contrary to popular belief, studies have shown that being hard on ourselves will not cause us to become more successful or effective. In fact, being accepting and kind toward ourselves lays the ground for sustainable change. We will explore this in greater detail in the next chapter on self-compassion. As someone who always seeks to better herself, this was something I struggled with, since I believed that if I only did more or pushed myself harder, I would love myself to a greater degree. The truth is that loving ourselves means releasing self-judgement, allowing ourselves to make mistakes, and trusting that we will stand by ourselves no matter what happens. Here are 15 ways to help you break the cycle of self-judgment:

15 Ways to Release Self-Judgement:

1. Notice judgmental thoughts
2. Become mindful of your body's response
3. Identify the judgement's origin
4. Observe the situation as an outsider
5. Get comfortable with your emotions
6. Remember no one is perfect
7. Set realistic expectations

8. Stop overgeneralizing
9. Don't let thoughts turn into action
10. Respond differently
11. Stop using *"should, must, have to"*
12. Speak gently to yourself
13. Cut out toxic people
14. Make peace with the past
15. Appreciate yourself

Moving from a place of judgement also means shifting to a point of patience. In our increasingly fast-paced and busy world, patience is a virtue we could all benefit from now more than ever. We often talk about being accepting and patient toward others, but what about when it comes to ourselves? Self-patience is an essential self-love skill which can transform your relationship with yourself. When we place unrealistic expectations or needlessly pressure ourselves, it is not conducive to our growth or well-being. Instead, try trusting in yourself and the Universe's ability to provide your needs and see what happens! Here are 10 tips to help you become more patient with yourself:

10 Self-Patience Tips:

1. Be aware of your energy ebb and flow
2. Release the need to overthink or ruminate
3. Focus on progress over perfection
4. Embrace uncertainty
5. Remember you're doing the best you can
6. Avoid multitasking if possible
7. Practice self-control
8. Step away if you're feeling triggered
9. Give yourself a break
10. Define what "success" means to you

The ability to validate ourselves and our emotions cannot be underestimated in its capacity to promote acceptance and healing. Validating ourselves means accepting our internal experience with compassion and love. In this state, we do not judge or criticize ourselves, but rather hold space for ourselves. Interestingly, those who fail to validate their experience exhibit less emotional control, are more prone to mental health issues, and are more inclined to engage in impulsive behavior. Validating ourselves has the potential to improve our interpersonal skills and the quality of our relationships. Developing our emotional intelligence and connecting with our body's response can help us cultivate greater self-validation. Keep in mind that self-validation should not be confused with self-approval which refers to a judgement of ourselves and our worth. Validating ourselves does not mean that we appraise or justify our thoughts or actions either. When we validate ourselves, we are basically saying, *"I see you and your feelings are valid."* Remember: you are not your failures or accomplishments, but the conscious awareness beneath it all. By acknowledging and validating ourselves, we are less likely to rely on positive feedback and the opinions of others, but instead turn to ourselves for reassurance and support. Here are 10 ways to help foster self-validation:

10 Ways to Validate Yourself:

1. Practice mindfulness
2. Identify your needs
3. Act intentionally
4. Engage in honest reflection
5. Normalize your thoughts and feelings
6. Encourage and support yourself
7. Speak to yourself as a friend
8. Acknowledge your progress
9. Recognize your efforts

10. Find joy from within

Humanist psychologist Dr. Carl Rogers once said, *"The curious paradox is that when I accept myself just as I am, then I can change."* Dr. Rogers developed the 3 Parts of the Self-Concept in order that we may fully accept and understand all the parts of ourselves. Your self-concept is how you perceive yourself, including the qualities, attributes, and behaviors that make up who you are. For example, *"I'm a natural artist"* or *"I'm shy and introverted"* etc. According to Dr. Rogers, the self-concept is comprised of three elements: the ideal self, self-image, and self-worth. The ideal self is the person we want to be and the qualities we are working toward exhibiting (ex. *"I'm an honest person"*). Self-image refers to how we perceive ourselves and the various social roles we play (ex. *"I'm a loving friend"*). Lastly, self-worth represents how much we accept and value ourselves (ex. *"I am inherently enough and worthy of my desires"*). Congruence symbolizes the level of balance we have between the three different parts of the self. When all three aspects are in alignment, we experience congruence, however if they do not overlap, we encounter incongruence.

For example, if our ideal self is self-assured and confident, yet we possess a poor self-image, there is discord within us which will negatively impact our self-worth. During my younger years, this used to be an area of internal conflict for me. In middle school, I wanted to be "cool" and "aloof" like my peers, yet since the day I was born, I've always had a lively and enthusiastic personality. I wore my heart on my sleeve and I didn't try to pretend to be something I wasn't. I would (and still do) get excited by everything and I don't put on airs. Since my ideal self and self-image were different, I struggled with my self-concept during those formative years. It wasn't until later on when I began to fully accept myself, that I experienced congruence with regard to my self-concept.

3 Elements of Self-Concept

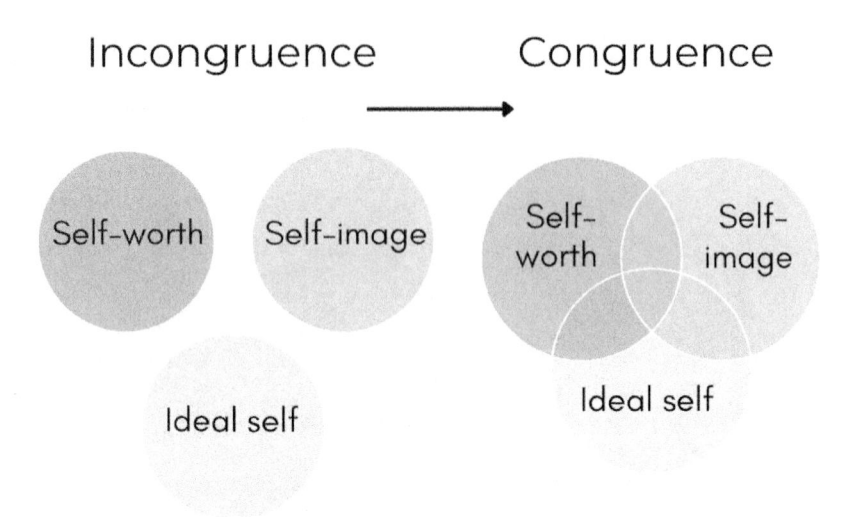

Incongruence → Congruence

Self-worth   Self-image

Ideal self

Self-worth   Self-image

Ideal self

Dr. Carl Rogers (1959)

Fortunately, the self-concept is not fixed and can change depending on the people we interact with in our lives. This is why it is crucial to spend time with individuals who are supportive and bring out the best in you. The concept of self is fluid and ever-evolving, always providing room for growth. When our self-concept is strong, we are less likely to be influenced by the negative opinions of others. With regard to self-concept, the goal is to achieve balance within our respective parts as this will lead to self-actualization, which will be fully discussed in Chapter 9. Dr. Rogers also outlines the 7 character traits of a fully functioning person which is described as an individual who has an awareness and acceptance of themselves and the world around them:

Dr. Carl Rogers's 7 Characteristics of a Fully Functioning Person:

1. Embraces new experiences
2. Creative and spontaneous
3. Lives in the present moment
4. Adaptable and flexible
5. Trusts themselves and their capabilities
6. Possesses the freedom to make their own decisions
7. Leads a multifaced existence (acceptance of all emotions)

To conclude this section, let's examine the difference between body positivity and body acceptance which are often used interchangeably. To keep it simple: body positivity is approving of our bodies and body acceptance means accepting our bodies just as they are. Before we can love and appreciate our bodies, we must first accept all of ourselves including the parts we have mislabeled as "unattractive" or "not good enough." Society places unrealistic and often harmful expectations on how we should look which can lead to low self-worth, self-doubt, and insecurities. The interesting thing is that physical beauty is actually an illusion and a social construct which periodically changes throughout history and among various cultures. I remember reading the bestselling book, *The Beauty Myth: How Images of Beauty Are Used Against Women*, in my undergraduate career and the profound impact it had on my perceptions of beauty. In the book, author Naomi Wolf analyzes the *beauty myth* which has been used to oppress women for centuries. The beauty myth is, "*an obsession with physical perfection that traps the modern woman in an endless spiral of hope, self-consciousness, and self-hatred as she tries to fulfill society's impossible definition of 'the flawless beauty.'*" Ugh, how many years of my youth did I waste trying to achieve a perfection that does not exist! Imagine if we spent as much time obsessing over our bodies as we did on caring and nurturing ourselves. The book explains how the mass media and beauty industry play on women's fears and insecurities by promulgating unrealistic standards of beauty to keep women buying and consuming. Great for capitalism, not so great for our body image, right?

It's so easy for our self-image to plummet based on society's distorted beauty standards. Body acceptance allows us to separate our self-worth from our appearance and accept our bodies as they are, free of judgement. From this perspective, we do not view our body as a problem to be fixed, but rather a vehicle for our inner essence. Body acceptance means recognizing that our value does not lie in our physical appearance. Understanding that our body does not require approval or validation can be truly empowering. Without the judgement and shame, we are more likely to make healthier choices and honor our body's needs. Here are 10 ideas to help promote body acceptance:

10 Body Acceptance Tips:

1. Follow body-positive social media accounts
2. Unfollow or mute pages that make you feel bad
3. Question your beauty beliefs and standards
4. Stop comparing yourself to others or a past version of yourself
5. Ditch the scale and focus on your health instead of weight
6. Move your body in ways that feel good
7. Eat intuitively and don't deprive yourself
8. Choose clothes that fit your body and style
9. Only speak kind words about your body or anyone else's
10. Surround yourself with loving and supportive friends

Fully accepting yourself looks like:

- Focusing on your strengths and positive qualities

- Allowing yourself to make mistakes with grace and compassion
- Embracing your imperfections
- Releasing perfectionism
- Letting go of people-pleasing
- Accepting the things in life you cannot change
- Validating your feelings & experiences
- Starting a gratitude journal
- Acknowledging your achievements
- Celebrating your accomplishments

Activity #1:

Self-Acceptance Sentence Frames

Instructions: For each of the following sentences, fill in the blank spaces below with words of acceptance, kindness, and love:

1. I can't change_____ about myself, so I choose to embrace it

2. My top 3 strengths are: _____, _____, and _____

3. I choose to release_____

4. It's time to forgive_____

5. I will no longer compare myself to_____

6. I will stop worrying about_____

7. Even though I_____, I love and accept myself

8. I deserve _____in my life

9. Today I will celebrate myself by_____

10. I'm thankful for_____

Activity #2:

Achieving Congruence

Instructions: Select an area of your life in which you are struggling (ex. body image, self-talk, etc.) and draw 3 circles labeled, *"Ideal Self," "Self-Image"* and *"Self-Worth."* For each category, write down how you want to feel (ideal self), how you view yourself (self-image), and how it is impacting your self-worth.

Activity #3:

Acceptance in Action

This activity is intended to help you accept the areas in your life which are within or without your control.

Instructions: Draw two circles inside of each other. In the center circle, write down 5 things you can control. In the outer circle, list 5 things you cannot control. Reflect on how you can focus more on what is within your control and release what is outside of your control:

Things outside my control:

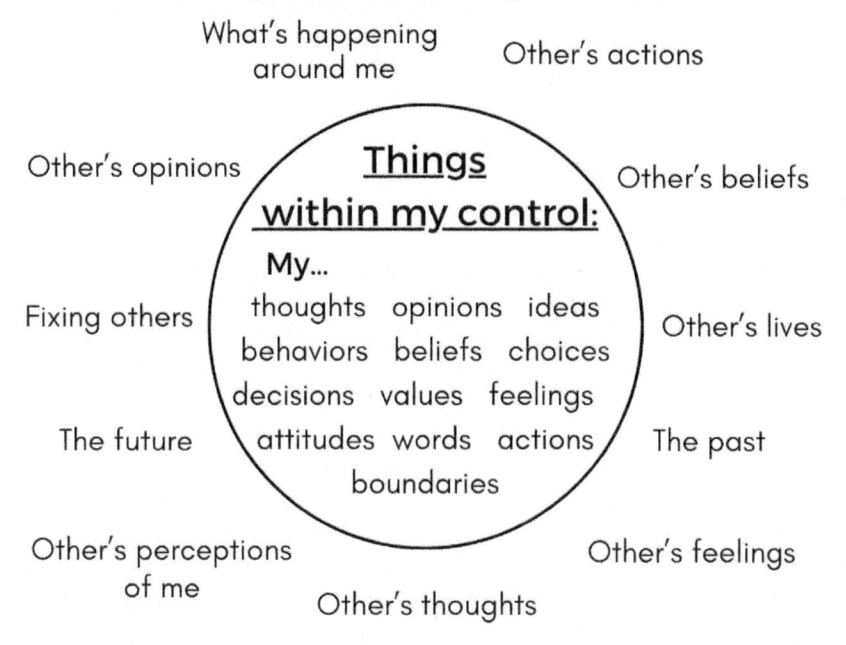

What's happening around me

Other's actions

Other's opinions

Other's beliefs

Fixing others

Other's lives

The future

The past

Other's perceptions of me

Other's feelings

Other's thoughts

Things within my control:

My...
thoughts opinions ideas
behaviors beliefs choices
decisions values feelings
attitudes words actions
boundaries

Step 4

Practice Self-Compassion (Self-Compassion)

"If your compassion does not include yourself, it is incomplete"
-Jack Kornfield

Seviana's Story Part 1

"This needs to be taught in schools!" my client Seviana exclaimed one day during a session together. She was referring to self-love and offering ourselves self-compassion when we are suffering. Seviana is beautiful inside and out with a heart of gold, but her insecurities and lack of self-worth were preventing her from owning her power and fully shining her light on the world. She is sweet and bubbly with a cheerful disposition. Even though she was my youngest client, she has an old soul and is wise beyond her years. Seviana struggled with effectively expressing her emotions and a lack of confidence. She recognized that she did not value herself which was trickling into the other areas of her life. She regularly experienced self-doubt and didn't feel good enough. Seviana longed for a sense of inner peace and to be in control of her emotions, but she lacked the tools to do so. When Seviana would get upset, she would respond in anger and later regret her initial reaction. She also questioned her capabilities and she constantly

worried how others perceived her. Seviana felt uncertain about herself which was impacting every aspect of her life. Her inner critic had taken control and her negative thoughts were weighing her down.

Upon completion of the program, Seviana became more mindful of her triggers and is better able to control her outbursts. Today, she practices mindfulness and remaining in the present moment which has increased her self-confidence. Seviana began challenging her limiting thoughts and replacing them with more accurate beliefs. She no longer believes everything she thinks, but rather questions if her thoughts are true or false. Her family relationships have improved and Seviana experiences a deeper appreciation for her life. Today, she speaks to herself with a sense of grace and compassion. Seviana feels confident and self-assured in her ability to navigate the stresses of life. A whole new world has opened up for her. She is truly the captain of her ship.

As you can see, Seviana's story is a perfect example of the power that speaking kindly and compassionately to ourselves has on improving our lives. How we speak to ourselves greatly impacts the quality of our existence. It has been said that, *"our word is our wand,"* which means that our words have the potential to create magic or destruction in our lives. At this point in your journey, you hopefully possess a deeper awareness of who you are and you are on the road to accepting yourself. For this next step, we will be observing your self-talk and ways in which you can demonstrate more self-compassion in your life.

Self-kindness and self-compassion are at the core of self-love. These two terms are often used synonymously, but in actuality self-kindness is treating yourself like a friend and self-compassion involves giving yourself grace and empathy when you are struggling. Without them, it is impossible to truly love and appreciate yourself. In this chapter, I will be referencing the work of self-compassion researcher Dr. Kristin Neff whose book, *Self-Compassion: The Proven Power of Being Kind to Yourself*, has been instrumental on my own and many of my client's self-love journeys. Dr. Neff defines self-compassion as: *"extending compassion to one's self in instances of perceived inadequacy, failure, or general suffering."* How profound is that! Self-compassion does not mean only loving ourselves when everything is going right, but offering ourselves grace and compassion when we are struggling and need it the most. It is the salve to our emotional wounds and connects us to our shared humanity. In addition, we will discuss the necessity of self-kindness which provides us the opportunity to see ourselves as a beloved friend who we value and cherish. We will also consider the importance of reframing our thoughts, using positive self-talk, and incorporating affirmations in this chapter. Finally, we will wrap up the section by observing the impact of forgiving ourselves on the path of self-compassion.

According to Dr. Neff, there are 3 elements of self-compassion: mindfulness, self-kindness, and common humanity. When we are mindful, we witness our thoughts without judgment or suppressing difficult emotions. An essential aspect of mindfulness is being aware of the emotions we are experiencing without identifying with them but rather allowing them the space to be. We do not resist, repress, or overexaggerate what we are feeling in those difficult moments. Self-kindness involves practicing a non-judgmental attitude and offering ourselves the same warmth and understanding we would to a friend who was suffering. It is critical that we speak to ourselves with kindness no matter what is happening around us. Lastly, common humanity means acknowledging that we all suffer and make mistakes as part of our shared humanity. We are all inexplicably connected.

3 Elements of Self-Compassion

1. Mindfulness
Acknowledge that this is a moment of suffering. Observe your thoughts without judgement

2. Self-kindness
Be kind and supportive to yourself as you would a friend

3. Common Humanity
Remind yourself that we all struggle and no one is perfect

Dr. Kristin Neff (2015)

It is a common misconception that being hard on ourselves will make us more successful. Ironically, studies show that we are generally more effective when we practice self-compassion. When we shame and beat ourselves up, we make progress harder. Dr. Neff notes that showing ourselves compassion allows us to reach our highest potential and live a more fulfilling life. When we acknowledge our struggles, we are able to move past them more quickly. Self-compassion is the antidote to self-criticism and here's why: studies show that self-compassion has been proven to-increase motivation, boost happiness, improve body image, enhance self-worth, foster resilience, and lower psychological distress. On the other hand, criticizing ourselves will likely reduce motivation and make progress less obtainable.

Self-esteem and self-compassion are often used interchangeably, however there are major distinctions between the two which Dr. Neff highlights in her book. Our goal is to focus more of our attention on cultivating self-compassion and less on developing self-esteem, and here's why: self-esteem evaluates our worth compared to other people, is contingent on external circumstances, and is often fluctuating, while self-compassion holds space for our personal inadequacies, is an internal state of being, and is typically more stable. Self-esteem is based on our accomplishments and successes whilst forcing us to hide our inadequacies. Conversely, self-compassion does not require us to hide who we are and is always available to us. For example, if someone loses their job, the person operating from self-esteem will likely feel bad about themselves and perhaps question their self-worth, yet the person engaging in self-compassion will allow themselves to feel their feelings and give themselves positive reassurance. It may seem like a minor shift, yet it can make all the difference. In the midst of stress and overwhelm, Dr. Neff provides a simple, yet effective 3-Step Self-Compassion Break:

3 Step Self-Compassion Break:

Step 1: *"This is a moment of suffering"*

Take a moment to become mindful of the feelings you are experiencing and label them without identifying with your emotions (ex. *"this is challenging"* or *"I'm feeling scared"* etc.).

Step 2: *"Suffering is a part of life"*

Remind yourself that suffering is part of the human condition and we all go through difficult times. Connecting with your common humanity can help you feel less alone (ex. *"everyone makes mistakes"* or *"other people feel this way too"* etc.).

Step 3: *"May I be kind to myself"*

In a calm and gentle manner, speak to yourself as you would a friend. Repeat a loving mantra for when you are struggling. Check in with yourself to see what it is you truly need (ex. words of encouragement, forgiving yourself, reaching out to someone, etc.).

Being able to correctly recognize and label our emotions is a key component of self-compassion. How can we give ourselves what we need if we don't know what we are experiencing? We do not identify with our feelings, but rather are the silent observer who is aware of what is actually going on. It is also crucial to become more aware of our words. For example, *"I'm anxious"* and *"I feel anxious"* are two completely different statements. The former implies that *I am* what I'm experiencing, yet the latter indicates that this is a passing and transitory state. Self-compassion means giving way to *all* of our emotions without shame or judgement and offering ourselves sincere kindness and understanding.

Why is it easy to treat a friend with love and kindness, yet it can be so challenging to treat ourselves in the same way? Becoming your own best friend is a self-love must. Self-kindness encourages us to engage with ourselves in a supportive and friendly manner. As mentioned earlier, you are your longest and most consistent relationship. The key to building a healthy relationship with yourself is being gentle with yourself and becoming your own safe place. This involves connecting with yourself on a deeper level and taking care of your wants and needs. Here are 10 simple ways to become your own bestie:

10 Ways to Be Your Own Bestie:

1. Get to know yourself
2. Always have your own back

3. Praise and compliment yourself
4. Be honest with yourself
5. Value your opinion the most
6. Take yourself on a solo date
7. Learn to have fun on your own
8. Embrace your uniqueness
9. Commit to your growth
10. Do a random act of kindness for yourself

Reframing your thoughts is a helpful self-compassion skill that anyone can cultivate. When we reframe, we take something and look at it from a different perspective. Positive reframes are essential when speaking to ourselves. For instance, an incident can occur yet what matters the most is the *story* we tell ourselves about what happened. Here's an example: let's say that you are at a party and you end up spending the evening with your friend Maddy instead of chatting with other people. From a limited or negative mindset you might tell yourself, *"No one likes you. You didn't connect with any new people. You are so awkward! Why can't you be more outgoing and sociable?"* However, reframing the event might look like, *"Wow, Maddy must really care about me and our friendship to hang out with me all night. I really am an excellent listener and a kind friend. I have so much to give others."* Don't get me wrong: I am by no means saying that this is easy, but if there are contrasting ways to perceive the exact same situation, why not focus on the possibility that feels better? It's usually the truth!

Speaking to yourself in an encouraging and supportive way is a self-love essential. Negative self-talk can cause self-doubt, unnecessary stress, and is detrimental to our self-worth. On the other hand, positive self-talk improves our confidence, encourages healthy habits, strengthens our relationships, decreases anxiety and depression, and enhances our resiliency and our ability to cope. Speaking positively to ourselves also improves performance and makes us more effective. Titan of industry Henry Ford once said, *"Whether you think you can, or you think you can't – you're right."* What a difference how we speak to ourselves can make! This inner dialogue cannot be underestimated in its ability to determine the course of our lives.

Our internal narrative is a mixture of unconscious and conscious thoughts. As mentioned earlier, 90% of our thoughts are unconscious. Therefore, the key is to become more aware of our inner voice and how we talk to ourselves. Consequently, we can counter any self-defeating thoughts with a more realistic approach. The mind often cannot tell the difference between what is real or imagined which can be used to our advantage. It is also important to notice what your thoughts are trying to tell you. For example, if you are single and feel bad after spending time with your married friends, you may hold some unconscious thoughts and fears surrounding your ability to find romantic love. If you would like to improve the way you speak to yourself, here are 10 positive self-talk tips:

10 Positive Self-Talk Tips:

1. Become aware of your inner dialogue
2. Analyze your thoughts
3. Question self-limiting beliefs
4. Regularly check-in with your emotions
5. Be conscious of your environment and triggers
6. Look for the silver lining
7. Practice gratitude
8. Speak positively to others
9. Spend time with uplifting people
10. Visualize the best possible outcome

Incorporating affirmations can be an excellent way to show yourself more kindness and compassion. Affirmations are basically positive statements that you repeat to yourself throughout the day to challenge the negative chatter with more empowering beliefs. Using affirmations can be a tool to help rewire your brain and create new neural pathways. Please note: I always stress to my clients that the affirmation must be something that is not too much a stretch and is somewhat believable. For example, if someone hates their body, it is probably best not to start out with affirming, *"I love my body"* but rather something like, *"I appreciate all my body does for me"* and go from there. Just like anything else, you have to feel it to believe it! My favorite affirmation is: *"I am capable"* since it reminds me that whatever it is I want to manifest in my life, I hold the key and so do you. During times of uncertainty and distress, it is easy for the mind to spiral and for unease to set in. Sometimes life throws us for a loop and we are not sure where to go or what to do next. We all encounter challenges and obstacles on the journey of life, but what is crucial is possessing the tools to handle whatever happens in an encouraging and supportive manner. Learning to self-soothe and comfort ourselves is a necessary skill to get us through life's inevitable ups and downs. Developing resiliency and the ability to cope can reduce unnecessary struggling and suffering. Here is a list of 20 short and sweet positive affirmations to have on hand for those difficult moments:

20 Empowering Affirmations:

1. *"I am capable of handling whatever life throws my way"*
2. *"I am in control of my life"*
3. *"I believe in myself and my abilities"*
4. *"I accept and love myself as I am"*
5. *"Everything is going to be okay"*
6. *"I'll take this one day at a time"*

7. *"I am stronger than I realize"*
8. *"I can do hard things"*
9. *"Doing my best is enough"*
10. *"I will get through this"*
11. *"I can relax and let go"*
12. *"I can ask for help if I need it"*
13. *"I have the power to change my life"*
14. *"These feelings will pass"*
15. *"This won't last forever"*
16. *"It's okay to make mistakes"*
17. *"I've survived worse than this"*
18. *"I am making progress"*
19. *"I've done this before and I can do it again"*
20. *"Everything will work out for my highest good"*

Is there anything you haven't forgiven yourself for? Self-love is not possible if we keep berating ourselves for the mistakes in our past which hinder our ability to start over again. We will conclude this chapter on the topic of self-forgiveness, along with tips to release any internal judgment you may be harboring against yourself. Refusing to forgive ourselves for something that already happened is like carrying around heavy luggage that is wearing us down. This is your sign that it is time to let it go! We all deserve a fresh start. It is not to say that we do not take responsibility for our actions and make amends if possible. If we sincerely learn from our mistakes, it can allow us to grow and develop in ways we had never imagined. As the great Maya Angelou once said, *"When you know better, you do better."* Forgiving ourselves is a necessity for our mental, emotional, and physical health and well-being. Lack of self-forgiveness has been linked to anxiety, depression, and a weakened immune system. Marriage and Family

Counselor Keir Brady outlines the 7 essential steps for practicing self-forgiveness which I have found to be the most helpful:

7 Self-Forgiveness Steps:

1. Define Forgiveness

Depending on how you were raised, the term can be quite broad, so define what forgiveness means to you. Forgiveness does not mean forgetting or condoning an action, but it does include acknowledging what happened and taking responsibility if appropriate. Forgiveness may mean that when you make a mistake, you recognize it is okay not to be perfect and you do not berate yourself for your shortcomings. Instead, you choose to learn and grow from the experience while showing yourself compassion. This can also be an opportunity to connect with your common humanity. You can remind yourself that no one is perfect and we all make mistakes (ex. *"forgiveness involves taking ownership of my part and making amends for what I did by sincerely apologizing"*).

2. Acknowledge your Feelings

As mentioned earlier, identifying and labeling our emotions can help us move through them more quickly. A variety of emotions may be present and that is completely normal. Feel free to use the Emotions Wheel at the end of the chapter. It is important that you allow yourself to experience whatever comes up (ex. sadness, shame, guilt, etc.) free of judgement, wallowing, or rumination. This is an opportunity to gain a deeper understanding of what happened so that you can move past denial or regret (ex. *"I feel ashamed for how I treated her and I'm angry at myself for not doing better at the time. I recognize that these feelings are difficult, but they will pass"*).

3. *Acknowledge your Part*

In this step, you own your part in the situation and take responsibility for your words and actions. Please note: this is not an excuse to criticize or judge yourself, but rather a chance to take your power back and focus on what you can control. Understanding why you acted how you did will make you less inclined to again moving forward. When we learn from our mistakes, we are more likely to make better choices in the future. Self-sabotage, denial, and judgement hinder true progress (ex. *"what I said was hurtful. Next time, I will be more careful with my words"*).

4. *Apologize*

Next, you apologize or make amends to whoever you may have harmed. If this is not possible, write a letter to this individual but do not send it. You cannot control how another person will react or whether they decide to forgive you, yet you will have the peace of mind that you did everything in your power to make matters right. Remind yourself that you did your best and that is all any of us can do. You can also write yourself an apology letter for not treating yourself as you should have in the past. In your apology, be sure to include what you did, why you regret it, address the pain it may have caused, and what you will do differently next time (ex. *"Allie, I am so sorry I implied that there was something wrong with you. In the moment, I was triggered but I now realize that what I said was cruel and untrue. I regret causing you any pain and damaging our friendship. You mean a lot to me and I feel terrible for making you feel bad in any way. I promise that if I'm ever triggered again, I will express how I'm feeling and not lash out. I am truly sorry. Will you please forgive me?"*).

5. *Learn from the Experience*

This is an opportunity to reflect on the experience and what you learned so that you are less likely to do it again in the future. In this step, you recognize that your behavior has consequences which affect others. Every situation teaches us something about ourselves and an area of growth we can cultivate and develop. For instance, most of us become more irritable when we are stressed, haven't eaten, or slept properly. Becoming aware of your triggers can also provide a deeper understanding of your common responses and reactions. Instead of getting caught up on what you did "wrong," you can focus your attention on what you can do differently moving forward (ex. *"I snapped at Allie because I've been feeling unsatisfied in my marriage and overwhelmed at work lately. This experience taught me that I was projecting my own unhappiness on her and there are some things in my life that I want to change"*).

6. *Make Meaningful Changes*

In this step, you make the necessary adjustments and modifications to your behavior. If changing your behavior won't fix the situation, you engage in something purposeful such as: serving others, sharing your story, working toward a solution, etc. In the example above, the first friend will now be more conscious of her triggers and considerate of how she communicates with her friend, Allie. She will no longer behave as she had previously done in future interactions (ex. *"I'm feeling uncomfortable discussing this. Do you mind if we change the topic?"*).

7. *Practice Compassion*

What a perfect way to complete this chapter and come full circle! As we covered, self-compassion can serve to heal us from the inside out. In this final step, you acknowledge and validate the difficult work you have completed while offering yourself grace and compassion. You separate yourself from the mistake and remind yourself that you are inherently worthy and loved. Additionally, you recognize that these constructive changes will benefit your growth and relationships (ex. *"it was hard for me to be vulnerable with Allie, but I'm glad I did because it has made our friendship stronger and brought us closer together. In the past, I would have replayed the incident over and over again in my head, but now I can release it and forgive myself"*).

Practicing self-compassion looks like:

- Developing a mindfulness routine (ex. meditation, nature walk, etc.)
- Creating a self-love ritual
- Listening to your body and intuition
- Incorporating self-love affirmations
- Speaking gently and patiently to yourself
- Reframing "failures" as learning opportunities
- Releasing the need to overthink
- Becoming aware of how to self-soothe and comfort yourself
- Labeling your thoughts and moods without identifying with them
- Checking in with yourself throughout the day and taking breaks

Activity #1:

Compassionate Self-Talk Exercise

Instructions: Based off the following scenarios, respond to yourself how you would to a close friend:

1. You didn't get the job you applied for that you really wanted

2. You are driving and accidentally cut someone off and they are honking at you
3. You make a mistake at a party and feel embarrassed
4. You missed an important deadline at work
5. You disappointed someone close to you

Activity #2:

Content Reframing

This activity is drawn from narrative psychology which suggests that we give our stories meaning which shapes our identity.

Instructions: Choose an incident or experience which has caused you to feel ashamed, insecure, or bad about yourself and answer the following questions:

1. Is there a different story that you could tell yourself about what happened?
2. What has the experience taught you?
3. How has it helped you to grow?
4. How can you use what you learned to help others?
5. How has it positively contributed to the person you are today?

Activity #3:

Emotions Wheel

Instructions: Using the Emotions Wheel, write down at least 5 feelings you have experienced today and the context in which they showed up. Did you identify with your feelings? Why or why not? What do you believe your emotions were trying to tell you? How can you best honor your feelings?

Emotions Wheel

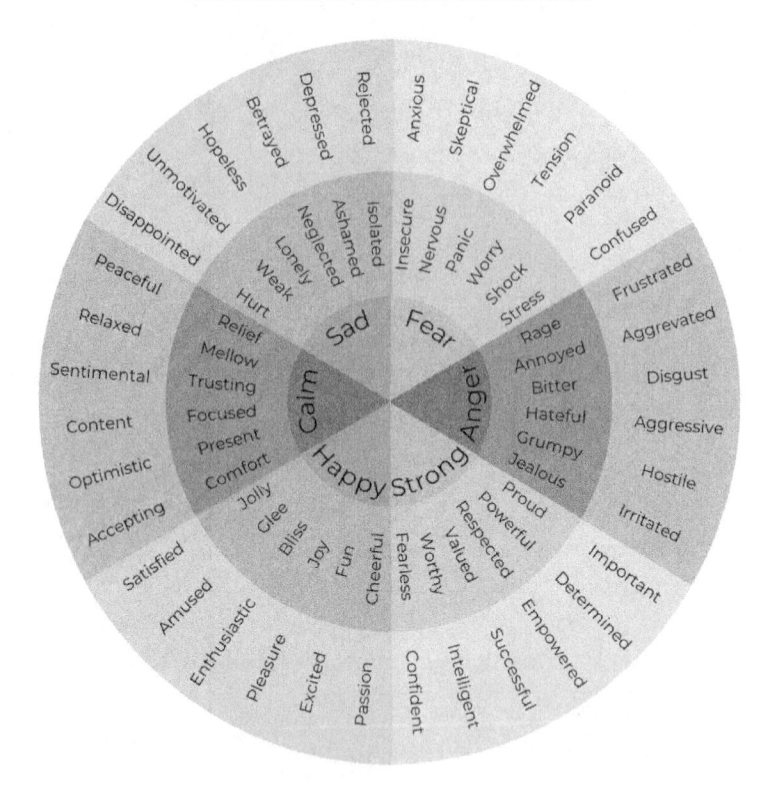

Step 5

Heal Your Past (Self-Healing)

"Your wound is probably not your fault, but your healing is your responsibility" -Denice Frohman

A major aspect of learning to love ourselves is addressing and healing the limiting beliefs we have experienced. It is having the courage and vulnerability to face our fears, heal our traumas, and release the past so that we can write a new story. The first step to healing your past is recognizing any limiting beliefs you may have. The purpose of this chapter is to reconnect you to your true self and to help you let go of the limiting beliefs that have been holding you back in your life. In this section, we will look at inner child healing, which includes childhood wounds and trauma responses. We will also explore two inner child healing stories that demonstrate the transformative nature of this work in healing our lives. Additionally, we will examine attachment styles as well as the barriers to healthy relationships which are: codependency, attracting unavailable partners, toxic relationships, and unhealthy communication styles. Next, we will discuss the 12 elements of a healthy relationship. Finally, we will wrap up the chapter by analyzing the positive effects of narrative therapy in healing our past.

To begin, let's consider what limiting beliefs are and how they influence our lives. Limiting beliefs are false thoughts that are restrictive and hold us back in some way. They are basically lies we tell ourselves about ourself and the world. It is so easy to take our limiting beliefs as facts. Since the vast majority of our thoughts are unconscious, we may not even fully realize how many of our thoughts are untrue. Many people ignore or repress the limiting stories they have about themselves. They unconsciously repeat the beliefs in their mind and do not take action. The world is our mirror and our lives are a reflection of the beliefs we hold about ourselves and others. When we take responsibility for our lives, it is truly freeing and empowering. Limiting beliefs are often passed down from our family, community, and through the media. Overtime, we begin to identify with them and they become part of our story. When it comes to limiting beliefs, the stronger the belief, the more evidence we find to support it. This can manifest itself into different rules for others than ourselves (ex. *"other people deserve to find true love but I don't"*). Fortunately, coping strategies are clues. What we try to prove to the world can be a sign of an opposite belief we are defending against or overcompensating for. For instance, someone who is a people-pleaser or perfectionist may believe that they are not inherently good enough and are hustling to prove their worth. When limiting beliefs are left unaddressed, they can silently influence our lives as we will examine later on in this chapter.

First developed by Dr. Carl Jung, the inner child refers to the part of our psyche that is innocent and vulnerable and the subconscious messages we received in childhood which continue to influence our adult decisions. In his groundbreaking book, *Healing Your Lost Inner Child*, psychotherapist Robert Jackman explains the importance of inner child healing on our overall health and well-being. We cannot make peace with the past until we have addressed our repressed emotions and our painful memories. Inner child healing involves recognizing and validating the emotionally painful or traumatic experiences from childhood. This trauma often resides in the unconscious mind and if it is not healed may show up in the adult life as fears, phobias, or life patterns. Often times when we are struggling, it is related to unresolved childhood wounds. If your inner child is wounded, you may struggle with perfectionism, insecurities, self-criticism, people-pleasing, trust issues, abandonment issues, attracting unhealthy relationships, body image issues, sexual shame, etc. Bringing our unconscious core beliefs to the surface can be truly healing and empowering. If we want to create a new future, we must first understand our past. The following two charts outline common inner child wounds and trauma responses. Take a moment and see if there are any wounds or responses that resonate with you. This may be an area of your life which requires further healing. During inner child work, we dig deep to release the limiting beliefs that have been blocking you from manifesting your dreams and creating the life you deserve.

Inner Child Wounds

Abandonment

Fears being alone
People pleases
Co-dependent
Attracts emotionally unavailable people
Threatens to leave

Guilt

Feels ashamed and bad
Weak boundaries
Constantly apologizes
Passive communicator
Attracts people who make them feel guilty

Trust

Fears being hurt
Doesn't trust themselves
Feels insecure and needs external validation
Doesn't feel safe
Attracts people who make them feel unsafe

Neglect

Fears being vulnerable
Represses feelings
Easily angered
Struggles to say "no"
Low self-worth
Attracts people who don't appreciate or "see them"

@_jakewoodard (2022)

Trauma Responses

Flight	Fight
Over-thinker	Controlling
Workaholic	Anger outbursts
Perfectionist	Bullying behavior
Anxiety/panic/OCD	Manipulation
Avoidance	Narcissism
Trouble sitting still	Entitlement

Freeze	Fawn
Struggles with decisions	People-pleaser
Disassociating	Weak boundaries
Zoning out	Codependent
Brain Fog	Emeshment
Stuck	Loss of self
Isolating	Overwhelmed
Numb	

@ryanroseevans (2021)

Seviana's Story Part 2

"How is the work going so far?" I asked expectantly.

Long pause.

"I haven't started yet," Seviana replied sheepishly.

We were already two weeks into my 1:1 Radical Self-Love Coaching Program and my new client Seviana hadn't begun the materials I sent her. Anyone who has completed my program will tell you that it is intense and there is a lot covered. My approach is holistic so we consider all of the areas currently being affected by my client's lack of self-love and confidence. Seviana suffered from self-doubt and limiting beliefs that were standing in her way from living the life of her dreams. *"Maybe she's not ready?"* I thought to myself. A couple of months before I had promised her that, *"she would be Cinderella and I would be her fairy godmother helping make all of her dreams come true."* How was I able to do that if she didn't even want to take a look at the workbooks I had sent her? I was feeling discouraged but I knew there must be a reason for her hesitation. As discussed earlier, "The Refusal of the Call," is the second step in the Hero's Journey. Around this time, I sent Seviana a necklace (talisman) which ended up being a catalyst for her to share her reservations.

Seviana revealed that deep down she was afraid that she would not experience the self-love transformation that she was hoping for. She had been disappointed in the past and was concerned that she would not see results. If Seviana had not been open and vulnerable about her doubts and insecurities, she might have sabotaged herself from completing the program. Seviana was procrastinating her involvement in the program because of the limiting beliefs she had learned in childhood. Although she loves her father, they had a strained relationship and he would get upset with her for not finishing things that she had started. Seviana's procrastination was a defense mechanism and once we got to the root of it, she was able to move past her fears. She also struggled with perfectionism and was afraid that if her efforts weren't "perfect," she wouldn't reach her goals. Seviana's perfectionism stemmed from growing up as the "golden child" in her family and having unrealistic expectations placed upon her. She was the only one in her family to leave their small town and receive her college diploma. Due to the excess of attention, Seviana was perceived by some relatives as "entitled" and "spoiled." Seviana received numerous accolades and academic achievements, yet this only contributed to the pressure she put on herself. She was tired of seeking external approval and validation and hoped to release the need to please others.

During our time together, Seviana began healing her childhood wounds, setting healthy boundaries with others, valuing herself, and believing she deserved what her heart desired. Needless to say, she experienced the most profound breakthroughs and transformation of any clients I've witnessed. Seviana is not the same woman who started my program last year. When we first met, she struggled to make eye contact, lacked confidence in herself, and wrestled with body image issues. More than half of her closet was full of baggy shirts and clothes to hide her body. She felt anxious and uncomfortable about her appearance. After completing the program, Seviana no longer feels self-conscious, or the need to conceal herself, and finally feels good in her skin. Today, her wardrobe consists of feminine clothes and formfitting dresses that fit her personality to a tee. Seviana loves getting dolled up, wearing jewelry and makeup, and hitting the town. Allow me to clarify: I am not saying that all women need to fit some sort of feminine ideal, however I believe they should feel free to wear whatever they want and feel confident whilst doing it. Seviana basks in all of the attention she gets and recognizes her inherent worth. These days, she sends me pictures and videos of herself smiling confidently in her stylish outfits. She loves her body and no longer needs outside approval or validation. Seviana owns her power and is an unstoppable force to be reckoned with. Her gorgeous light shines from the inside out. I recently had the honor of meeting Seviana in person and I know she will be a life-long friend.

Incredible right? Seviana's experience is a brilliant demonstration of how healing your inner child can positively impact your adult life. It wasn't an easy journey, but Seviana's story is a perfect example of how when we do not heal our past, it can impact the present. Fortunately, we can do the healing work, which will alter the course of our future. Now let's check in again with my former client Sofia who experienced limiting beliefs that she learned as a child from her family:

Sofia's Story Part 2

When Sofia first reached out to me, she struggled with limiting beliefs, relationships, and the inability to feel satisfied with her life. Sofia didn't feel worthy and experienced a lack of self-love. She was raised in a chaotic, dysfunctional home and wanted to break the cycle of negative thinking. Her limiting thoughts were keeping her stuck in a cycle of fear and stopping her from living a fulfilling life. Sofia hoped to love herself more, feel a greater sense of security, and experience a positive and abundant mindset. In the beginning of our work together, Sofia was not even sure if change was possible, but she desperately wanted to believe her life could transform. She longed for something different from what she thought was attainable. Sofia was aware that she had limiting beliefs blocking her from reaching her full potential, yet she did not know how to heal and let them go. During our sessions, we got down to her core limiting beliefs and worked together to release them.

One of Sofia's major challenges was possessing a scarcity mindset. When it came to money and finances, she experienced blocks and resistance. This was not her fault, as she had been programmed at a young age to engage in fear-based thinking. Growing up, she formed limiting beliefs surrounding money and work. Sofia was taught that in order to be successful, one must work extremely hard at something they did not enjoy and sacrifice themselves for their occupation. These core beliefs were not always explicitly stated, yet she picked them up as a young girl. Children are like sponges that soak up the unconscious messages provided by their caregivers. During her childhood, she was not allowed to take up hobbies or engage in "frivolous" interests. Joy and excitement were just not a priority. Her parents did what they needed to do in order to survive, yet Sofia was in a position to be open to new possibilities and opportunities. Nevertheless, these old beliefs were preventing her from showing up fully in her life. As an adult, the same negative thoughts about herself and the world continued to arise even though they were not her actual beliefs. Deep down, she valued herself and her interests, but the old messages that she was being "selfish" or "irresponsible" kept creeping back into her mind. How could she know what she was passionate about if she hadn't had the chance to explore what was meaningful to her?

We worked together to heal her wounded inner child and challenge the core beliefs from her upbringing. An important aspect of Sofia's healing journey was bringing the unconscious limiting beliefs she was experiencing to light. It is very common to hold others responsible for the suffering in our past. Like so many, Sofia once blamed her family for her limiting beliefs, yet once she took accountability for her life, she was able to break free of the cycle that had been keeping her trapped. Part of her healing journey included discovering who she truly was and what was meaningful to her, regardless of her family's expectations. Sofia had the courage to move beyond what she believed was a "safe" career and consider what her life would be like if she broke the cycle of unhealthy generational patterns. This type of work is often difficult and uncomfortable, which is one of the reasons I am so proud of Sofia for sticking with it and not giving up. Sofia was eager to make the necessary changes in her life and she was enthusiastically proactive during our time together. Whenever she found something new that she was struggling with, she reached out to me for additional resources which I gladly provided. Sofia understood that if she showed up and did the work, she would experience results.

The last time we connected, she was taking new classes, investigating career options, and making time for the things that she found fulfilling. After working together, Sofia was able to relax more, release the need to be in control, and trust the flow of life. She began exploring things that she loved and taking up new hobbies. She now possesses an abundance mindset, believes the Universe has her back, and that life is working in her favor. Sofia recently received a pay raise and is experiencing the law of attraction firsthand. She is in control and no longer allows her past to determine her future. Sofia focuses on positivity, gratitude, and creating an abundant life. She is confident, self-assured, and ready to take on whatever life throws her way. As you can see, Sofia was able to heal her inner child and take her power back.

Inner child healing also considers our relationships with our primary caregivers and how they impact our current relationships. In their groundbreaking book, *Attached: the New Science of Adult Attachment and How It Can Help You Find-and Keep-Love*, authors Dr. Amir Levine and Rachel Heller explain how our unique attachment style impacts our relationships with others. According to Attachment Theory, the relationship children form with their primary caregiver(s) influences their ability to develop healthy bonds with others in adulthood. Our early bonds (or lack thereof) determine our attachment style and how we behave in relationships. Research demonstrates that these patterns continually show up in our connections with others (i.e. partners, children, friends, etc.). There are four types of attachment: secure, anxious, avoidant, and disorganized. Take the quiz to discover your unique attachment style:

https://www.attachmentproject.com/attachment-style-quiz/

Understanding your attachment style can help you form and maintain healthy relationships, release unhealthy patterns, ease anxiety and depression, and is related to our sense of self and emotional control. Our internal beliefs about love eventually manifest in the external world. Life is a mirror continually reflecting how we feel about ourselves. This is why it is essential that we let go of any limiting beliefs which do not serve us and believe we deserve blissful, fulfilling, and healthy relationships because that is what we will attract into our lives.

Attachment Styles

Secure
Comfortable with intimacy
Interdependent
Loving and trusting
Positive view of self/others

Anxious
Seeks excessive intimacy
Dependent
Positive view of others
Negative view of self

Avoidant
Avoids intimacy
Overly independent
Negative view of others
Positive view of self

Disorganized
Craves intimacy but fears it
Scared of rejection
Expects to be hurt
Negative view of self/others

Dr. Amir Levine & Rachel Heller (2011)

Once we are able to truly and more fully love ourselves, we are more inclined to call in friendships and relationships which benefit our highest good. Before we can do that, we need to examine a few of the barriers to healthy relationships which are codependency, attracting unavailable partners, toxic relationships, and unhealthy communication styles. Understanding our previous relationships allows us to heal the past and release negative patterns. It also makes space for the type of healthy and fulfilling relationships we deserve.

Popularized by author Melody Beattie in the 1980's, codependency refers to an unbalanced relationship where one individual puts their partner's needs ahead of their own, which can lead to enmeshment and relationship addiction. In a codependent relationship, boundaries are often blurred and one partner feels responsible for the emotions and behavior of the other. Over-functioning, enabling, fixing, controlling, people-pleasing, and rescuing are common signs of codependency. Codependents often feel that their self-worth is tied up in the relationship which they believe they cannot function properly without. Unfortunately, codependents tend to be narcissist magnets who only help to perpetuate an unhealthy relationship cycle. Codependency stems from childhood dysfunction or trauma, which is why it is necessary to heal our past from showing up in our current life. Although often referred to in romantic relationships, codependency can show up in any type of relationship. If you or someone you know struggles with codependency, here are some ways to help break the patterns of dependent behaviors:

10 Ways to Heal Codependency:

1. Put your needs first
2. Respect your own thoughts and opinions
3. Ask for what you need
4. Seek your own validation
5. Focus on what you can control
6. Set healthy emotional boundaries

7. Allow others to make their own choices
8. Develop a stronger sense of yourself
9. Become more self-reliant and independent
10. Prioritize your own goals and interests

Personally, I am all too familiar with the feeling of unrequited love. For those of you who are unfamiliar, unrequited love means loving someone who doesn't feel the same way. Ouch! Before I embarked on my self-love journey, I was constantly attracting men who were either unavailable or uninterested. I was unknowingly repelling the love that I sought due to my own limiting beliefs. Deep down, I was afraid of getting hurt and trying to protect myself, so I drew in men who *couldn't* break my heart because they were not a viable option. Unfortunately, this did not lessen the pain or heartache and in some ways exacerbated it. I didn't love or trust myself enough to know that I could handle whatever happened and I would be okay. As bestselling author and counselor Megan Logan notes, *"Women who struggle with self-love and insecurity often find themselves in the pursuer role."* This can show up as trying too hard or always being the one to reach out. Healing our relationships means recognizing that love shouldn't hurt or restrict us in any way. Remember: you are always deserving of respect, kindness, and reciprocal love.

Before we examine the elements of a healthy relationship, let's take a look at the warning signs of a toxic one. This may include a relationship with a coworker, family member, friend, partner, etc. Those who lack self-love can be unaware that certain behaviors are toxic and should be considered unacceptable in a relationship. Looking back on my former romantic partners, there are certain things I would never tolerate now which I had previously accepted as normal relationship dynamics. For example, I was often giving more than I was receiving and I did not feel seen, heard, or valued in these relationships. At the time, I was not conscious of these red flags which were eating away at my self-worth. Awareness and understanding are key for anyone who is in a relationship that makes them feel bad or disrespected. If you're currently involved in a toxic relationship, please consider reaching out to someone you trust for guidance and support. These are 20 signs of a toxic relationship:

20 Toxic Relationship Red Flags:

1. Envy or jealousy
2. Controlling or coercion
3. Judgmental attitude
4. Imbalance of power
5. Lack of trust or dishonesty
6. Manipulation or threats
7. Name-calling
8. Poor communication
9. Gaslighting
10. Neglect or exploitation
11. Disrespectful behavior
12. Infidelity
13. Constant drama or challenges
14. Consistent unreliability or uncertainty
15. Negative energy
16. Lack of support
17. Makes you feel unworthy
18. Feels uncomfortable
19. Leaves you unhappy or drained
20. Beneath your standards

Now let's compare the 4 main communication styles, 3 of which are considered unhealthy in long-term relationships. Unfortunately, people are not mind readers and generally do not know what we want or need unless we tell them. Healthy communication and having the ability to effectively express ourselves are the cornerstone of any successful relationship. Clearly expressing our thoughts, feelings, and needs not only strengthens the quality of our relationships, it also improves our relationship with ourselves. If we engage in unhealthy communication, it may mean that we lack confidence or self-worth. However, possessing a healthy communication style demonstrates that we value and respect ourselves and believe that we are deserving of a fulfilling relationship. Additionally, others are more likely to listen and hear us when we utilize healthy communication. In chapter 6, I will share helpful tips on how to foster assertive (healthy) ways of communicating with others, but for now here are the 4 main communication styles with examples:

4 Communication Styles:

1. *Passive*-the individual avoids expressing their thoughts and opinions; defers to the other person (ex. *"you decide"*).
2. *Aggressive*-the person imposes their will upon the other party; can be hostile (ex. *"we're doing it my way so get over it"*).
3. *Passive-aggressive*-the individual appears passive but is secretly upset (ex. the silent treatment).
4. *Assertive (healthy)*-the individual directly and honestly expresses themselves in a respectful manner (ex. *"I feel taken for granted"*).

Please note that this section is intended for communicating with our close friends and loved ones. Depending on the situation, it may be appropriate to use passive or aggressive communication to protect or keep ourselves safe. Always trust your gut instincts and act accordingly.

To wrap up this section on relationships, we will reflect on the key elements of a healthy relationship and why they are important. For those who grew up in a chaotic or dysfunctional home environment, it can be easy to identify what an unhealthy relationship looks like, yet it can be trickier to recognize how a healthy relationship can function. According to therapists Dr. Rachel O'Neill and Madeleine DiLeonardo, there are 12 signs of a healthy and mutually beneficial relationship to be on the lookout for:

12 Elements of a Healthy Relationship:

1. Trust
2. Mutual respect
3. Collaboration
4. Feeling of comfort
5. Sense of love and fondness
6. Healthy communication
7. Both partners needs are met
8. A sense of individuality
9. Authenticity
10. Confidence in how your partner feels
11. The ability to have hard conversations
12. You have fun together

To conclude this chapter, we will consider the benefits of narrative therapy in flipping the script of our lives. First developed in the 1980's by New Zealand-based therapists Michael White and David Epston, narrative therapy investigates the meaning behind the stories we tell ourselves about our life experiences and the ways in which they shape our identity. Narrative therapy allows an individual to be the objective expert in their life by separating themselves from their personal story in a non-judgmental way. It is similar to the Hero's Journey in that it empowers you to be the hero, not the victim of your story. Your personal narrative can offer deeper meaning and understanding into who you are which can be an optimal opportunity for healing and growth. Narrative therapy includes 4 main principles:

4 Principles of Narrative Therapy:

1. Reality is socially constructed and dependent on our interactions with others
2. Reality is influenced by and communicated through language
3. Having a narrative can help us organize and make sense of our reality
4. There is no "objective reality" or absolute truth; we all perceive things differently

Returning to Sofia's example, her beliefs surrounding money were shaped by her family's scarcity mindset which they had unconsciously communicated to her (ex. *"it is selfish to do what you want by making time for your interests"*). These limiting beliefs became part of her reality until she chose to question her core beliefs and perceive life in a more expansive light. Although it can be helpful to do this work with a therapist, there are 5 common narrative therapy tools which you can try out for yourself:

5 Narrative Therapy Techniques:

1. *Telling One's Story*

Retelling your personal narrative (ex. write down your story in order to find greater meaning and purpose behind your lived experiences).

2. *Externalization Technique*

Separating yourself from your behaviors or issues (ex. *"I am a sad person"* vs. *"sometimes I feel sad"*).

3. *Deconstruction Technique*

Breaking down problems into smaller issues (ex. *"I'm never going to find someone"* vs. *"maybe I can try putting myself out there more"*).

4. *Unique Outcomes Technique*

Taking a different perspective or viewpoint of the situation (ex. *"I really embarrassed myself at the party"* vs. *"everyone was so focused on what they were doing, I'm sure no one paid any attention"*).

5. *Existentialism*

Finding your own meaning and purpose in life (ex. defining what true joy and success mean to you).

Healing your past looks like:

- Writing your younger self a reassuring letter
- Releasing limiting beliefs you learned as a child
- Processing emotionally painful experiences
- Learning what your caregivers didn't teach you
- Reparenting and nurturing your adult self
- Letting go of unhealthy or abusive relationships
- Making peace with your inner critic
- Engaging in something fun and playful
- Forgiving someone who hurt you
- Learning to trust yourself and others

Activity #1:

My Life Story

Writing your life story can offer a sense of clarity and understanding into the events that make up your personal narrative. By reflecting on your significant life stages and experiences, you are offered the opportunity to weave together a more cohesive story. Additionally, this activity allows you to reestablish your identity by separating yourself from your past and taking a more objective point of view which can be truly healing and empowering.

Instructions: Respond to the following writing prompts based on your life thus far:

1. Write down the title of your book (ex. *"Jessica: A Story of Courage and Hope"*).
2. Write out a minimum of 7 chapters, each representing significant life stages and events (ex. *"Chapter 1: The Outcast-I was bullied in grade school but I didn't allow it to stop me from being who I am"*).
3. Write your final chapter and description (ex. *"Into the Future-my exciting travel adventures around the world"*).

Activity #2:

Challenging Limiting Beliefs

Choose at least one limiting belief about yourself that is negatively impacting your life (ex. *"I'm not capable"* or *"I'm not thin enough"* or *"I'm a burden to others,"* etc.) and answer the following questions:

1. What is the limiting belief?
2. Where did it originate?

3. Is there evidence to the contrary?
4. What is a more realistic belief?
5. What is one action step I can take as a result of this new belief?

Activity #3:

Flip the Script

Select a life challenge, disappointment, or failure and answer the following questions:

1. What did this teach me about myself?
2. What skills did I gain?
3. How can I be grateful for this experience?
4. What is something positive that came out of this situation?
5. How can I view this as a learning experience rather than a difficulty or failure?

Step 6

Know Your Worth
(Self-Worth)

"No one can make you feel inferior without your consent"
-Eleanor Roosevelt

Before we can step into the highest version of ourselves, we need to believe we are *already* inherently worthy and enough. This can prove challenging in a society that profits off of your deepest fears and insecurities while making you question yourself and your abilities. Knowing your worth means remembering who you truly are when everything external is stripped away. This includes your appearance, relationships, career, money, status, possessions, achievements, etc. One of my all-time favorite quotes is at the very end of the film, *The Wizard of Oz*, when Glinda the Good Witch turns to Dorothy and says, *"You had the power all along, my dear."* This quote reminds me that we have everything we need right in this moment and we hold the key to our own happiness. As discussed earlier, we cannot control what others do, yet we can establish healthy boundaries with ourselves and others.

In this chapter, we will explore the benefits of boundaries, as well as different forms and types of boundaries. We will also consider how self-sabotaging behaviors can lead to a lack of self-worth and tips for stopping the cycle of unhealthy actions. Additionally, we will examine our relationships with others in relation to boundaries, the need to people-please, and how to develop assertive communication. We will also look at the importance of self-advocacy in demonstrating our self-worth. Finally, we will discuss ways to connect you to your inherent self-worth and how to implement them. When you value yourself, you treat yourself with respect and refuse to settle for anything less than what you deserve. Remember: your self-worth is a non-negotiable and should never be conditionally based on someone or something else.

Yesterday, I found something I wrote in my early 20's before I had experienced the magic of self-love. At the time, my self-worth was tied up into being in a romantic relationship and I was pursuing one guy after the next, hoping someone would love and choose me. I felt incomplete without a partner and I wanted someone to validate my existence. The funny thing is that I was so interested in getting these young men to like me, that I never stopped to ask myself if I really cared for them and if they had the qualities that I was looking for in a partner. It is so easy to get caught up in the trap of seeking external love and forget that we *are* love and have the wonders of the Universe within us. Once I began to love and value myself as a whole and already complete person, I realized I was enough and I didn't need to prove myself to be deserving of love and happiness. I stopped seeking for someone to love me and instead started accepting and loving myself as I was which has made all the difference. I no longer feel like I need a relationship to "complete me," but that love in any form will benefit my life.

Let's begin by discussing boundaries as they are an integral part of self-love. Possessing healthy boundaries means that we honor our wants and needs while protecting our time, energy, and space. Boundaries encourage us to live in alignment with ourselves and not permit anyone to compromise or violate our values. If we lack boundaries with ourselves, it can lead to invalidating and self-sabotaging behaviors which we will consider later on. When we fail to set boundaries with others, it may lead to enmeshment, strained relationships, and resentment. We are also more inclined to attract one-sided relationships in which we are giving more time and energy than the other person. Trust me, I've been there! Our personal boundaries can help us determine what we will or will not accept in our relationships. Marriage and family counselor and author Sharon Martin outlines the ten benefits establishing healthy boundaries has in our lives:

10 Benefits of Setting Healthy Boundaries:

1. Enhances physical, mental, and emotional health
2. Reduces anxiety and stress
3. Helps prevent burnout
4. Lessens anger and resentment
5. Enhances assertiveness and confidence
6. Improves relationships
7. Deepens self-awareness
8. Increases compassion for others
9. Offers a deeper sense of personal safety and inner peace
10. Provides more time for what brings you joy

Boundaries can take on 3 specific forms: rigid, porous, and healthy. Let's take a look at the differences between the three:

Rigid boundaries

- Avoids intimacy
- Keeps others at a distance

- Extremely protective of personal information
- May appear aloof
- Rarely asks for help

Porous boundaries

- Overshares personal information
- Struggles with saying "no"
- Becomes too involved with other's lives
- Dependent on others
- May tolerate mistreatment

Healthy boundaries

- Values themselves
- Shares information appropriately
- Communicates effectively
- Doesn't compromise values or integrity
- Respects others

Healthy boundaries show that we respect and value ourselves. We do not over or under share personal information. We practice assertive communication and we express ourselves and our needs in a calm manner. These types of boundaries are essential in order to protect our energy and avoid burnout. Additionally, there are 6 types of boundaries which include: physical, intellectual, emotional, sexual, material, and time.

6 Types of Boundaries:

1. *Physical*-involve personal space and physical touch. What you do or don't do with your body

2. *Intellectual*-other people respecting your ideas, thoughts, and opinions
3. *Emotional*-respecting your own feelings and not oversharing with others
4. *Sexual*-clear communication, safety, and consent with regards to sex and intimacy
5. *Material*-involve money, possessions, & setting financial limits
6. *Time*-how you spend your time and who you spend it with

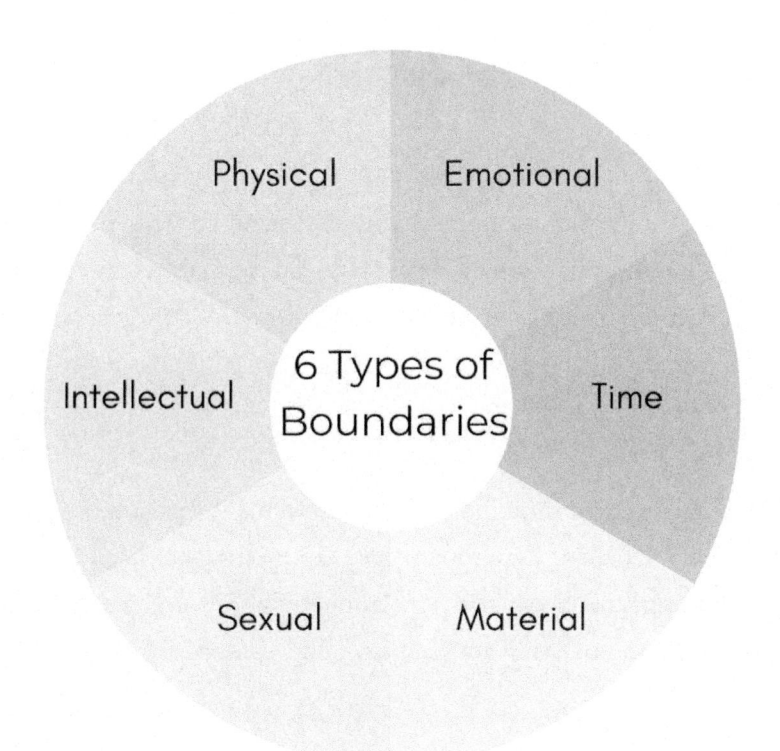

6 Types of Boundaries

- Physical
- Emotional
- Time
- Material
- Sexual
- Intellectual

Establishing healthy boundaries with ourselves can improve our overall health and well-being. If we have porous (weak) boundaries, we are more likely to engage in self-sabotaging behaviors. Self-sabotaging behaviors are harmful actions which undermine our progress and prevent us from achieving our goals and dreams. There are five types of self-sabotage which include: resisting change, procrastination, perfectionism, negative self-talk, and poor self-care. Often times when we are engaging in self-sabotaging behaviors, our minds are unconsciously doing what is familiar in order to keep us safe and protected which is why awareness is key. Later on in this section, we will examine a client story of how self-sabotage can be determinantal to self-love. Nationally recognized counselor Tanya Peterson outlines 5 simple tips that can help if you are engaging in self-sabotage:

5 Tips to Prevent Self-Sabotage:

1. *Acknowledge Unhealthy Patterns*

If you are constantly finding yourself engulfed in the same unhealthy or negative situations, it is crucial to become aware of any reoccurring themes (ex. eating junk food to comfort yourself every time you experience stress).

2. *Engage in Positive Self-Talk*

When a negative thought shows up, reframe it with a more realistic belief. Challenge your inner critic and remember not to believe everything you think (ex. validating how you are feeling overwhelmed and offering yourself love and compassion).

3. *Take Small Steps*

Tiny actions add up, so start out small. Reflect on the feelings associated with the self-sabotaging behavior and how it is harming you (ex. reminding yourself that when you eat too much junk food you feel bloated and don't sleep well).

4. *Develop Alternative Actions*

Write down 3 different ways of handling the situation that are in alignment with your values (ex. going for a walk, playing with a pet, eating a healthy snack, etc.).

5. *Identify and Embrace Your Strengths*

Focus on your personal strengths and capabilities when you are struggling (ex. write down 5 of your most admirable qualities).

Setting healthy boundaries with others is equally necessary for establishing our self-worth. When we value and respect ourselves, boundaries come more naturally. Lack of boundaries often leads to people-pleasing which is a major barrier to self-love. Interestingly enough, people-pleasing is actually a way to try and control other's perceptions of us and gain their approval. Therefore, if we validate ourselves, we will be less likely to people-please. When I didn't recognize my self-worth, I use to people-please and put other's needs before my own. This is so common and is something many of my clients have struggled with on their journey's as well. Other's happiness should not come at the expense of our own well-being. We are also not responsible for the emotions or behaviors of others. I used to constantly apologize for the smallest things and even situations I was not responsible for (ex. someone bumping into *me* at the supermarket). Personally, I've found that it is much more effective to thank others and show them appreciation rather than saying, *"I'm sorry"* all the time. For example, now if I'm running late to meet a friend, I'll say *"thank you so much for your patience. I really appreciate it,"* instead of apologizing profusely. Speaking our truth in a clear, confident, and composed manner is an excellent way to assertively communicate our wants and needs which is the ultimate act of self-worth. Here are 10 tips for using assertive *(healthy)* communication:

10 Assertive Communication Tips:

1. Know your limits
2. Refuse to compromise your values
3. Listen to your intuition
4. Be prepared and plan ahead of time
5. Use "I" statements
6. Clearly and kindly communicate your boundaries
7. Use confident body language
8. Be consistent and follow through on your decisions
9. Detach from the outcome
10. Remember that "no" is a complete sentence

Sam's Story Part 2

One of Sam's greatest wins occurred when she started setting healthy boundaries and practicing assertive communication. As you may remember, Sam battled with self-doubt and the inability to trust herself. In one of our first sessions Sam remarked, *"I don't open up to most people and it is a miracle I found you,"* which was a result of her trust issues. Because she lacked self-trust, it was difficult for her to get close to others. This is often the case when boundaries are weak and have yet to be properly established. Sam had been hurt in the past and her internal armor served to protect her from the abuse and mistreatment of other people. After working together, Sam began reaching out more and connecting with others. She finally trusted herself enough that she knew that she would have her own back and not allow others to overstep her boundaries.

During our sessions, one of Sam's major goals was to attain the inner peace which she longed for but had yet to fully achieve. In one of our last sessions together, I asked Sam what she needed more of to be at peace with herself and she replied that she was currently, *"experiencing the most peace"* she ever had. This was a result of her doing the work and setting healthy boundaries with herself and others. Once Sam learned to accept and trust herself, it was easier for her to implement appropriate boundaries in a variety of situations. She no longer puts herself down and in fact has begun advocating for herself. For example, recently a close friend made a cutting remark and instead of acting like it didn't bother her, Sam stood up for herself and calmly expressed how it made her feel. Sam has stopped worrying about what others think of her and she feels less self-conscious and more secure in herself. She also learned to stop sabotaging herself by establishing healthy boundaries and practicing self-care.

Additionally, Sam struggled for many years with guilt surrounding setting healthy boundaries at work. In her job as a manager of a large team, she was taking on way too much and cleaning up the messes of her staff. After completing the program, Sam now shares her expectations with her staff and sets healthy boundaries. She recently sent out an email to her team outlining their job descriptions as she was often having to do more work than was necessary. Sam used to work 60-80 hours a week and now she works less than 50 hours. This has contributed to a huge improvement in her job satisfaction. As she says, *"I am now #1 in my life,"* and she no longer experiences guilt when expressing her wants and needs. In our last session, Sam told me that she is, *"really happy and at peace with her life."* She feels that, *"the chains have been lifted,"* and she is truly free. Fortunately, Sam's partner was super encouraging and supportive during her self-love journey which helped to facilitate the process. He enjoyed watching her grow and blossom as she experienced a true self-love transformation. This is why it's essential to surround ourselves with loving and understanding individuals. There were times that she would stay up late into the night completing my workbook because as she said, *"I love it! It's so much fun,*

I couldn't put it down." Words cannot capture how proud I am of Sam for recognizing her inherent worth and taking her power back. She is a rock star!

Sam's story is an excellent example of advocating for ourselves. The ability to advocate for oneself is a defining marker of self-worth. Self-advocacy refers to the actions taken by an individual to communicate and assert their interests, wants, and needs. Advocating for yourself involves representing yourself and understanding your rights. It also includes making informed choices and taking responsibility for those decisions. Self-advocacy is an excellent way to empower yourself and demonstrate that you recognize your inherent worth. Advocating for ourselves can help us take control, effectively solve problems, and is something we can do literally anywhere! Here are 10 tips to help you advocate for yourself more effectively:

10 Self-Advocacy Tips:

1. Ask important questions
2. Learn how to get information
3. Don't assume anything
4. Practice active listening
5. Develop your communication skills
6. Articulate your needs
7. Be respectful, clear, and firm
8. Know your rights and responsibilities
9. Choose your battles wisely
10. Create a supportive network

Natalie's Story Part 1

Natalie is a stunning, highly intelligent, and successful mother of two teenage boys. Growing up in a visible and predominant family, there were many expectations placed upon Natalie from an early age and her self-worth stemmed from her appearance and achievements. She was a beautiful and talented child, yet the unwanted attention caused her to feel shy and self-conscious. Considering she was raised in the limelight, it made sense that she was so hard on herself, self-critical, and would scrutinize herself. Natalie didn't feel good enough and sought external validation which made it difficult for her to see her inherent worth and show up authentically. She struggled with body image issues, self-sabotage, and her self-worth. Natalie would engage in self-sabotaging behaviors such as not eating healthy, getting enough exercise, or sleeping well yet she couldn't understand why. During our time together, we delved deep into her unconscious limiting beliefs which were that if she played it "safe" and did not become the best version of herself, she could avoid the jealously and judgment of others that she was so accustomed to. Natalie was afraid to share her gifts and talents with the world, so she kept herself small in order to avoid the criticism of others, but in effect she was keeping herself stuck from moving forward with her dreams. If she created something, it would often be anonymous because she did not want the attention.

Natalie was also a narcissist magnet who attracted unhealthy relationships with men who objectified and used her. Men were drawn to her beauty, status, and wealth without getting to know and understand the real her. Unfortunately, this caused her to experience trust and abandonment issues in her romantic relationships. Natalie avoided vulnerability for fear of getting hurt as she had in the past. Her limiting beliefs surrounding relationships caused her to feel unworthy and undeserving of the men she truly desired. Even though she is beautiful, Natalie didn't feel attractive enough for the type of man she wanted to be in a relationship with. Her belief that she needed to look "perfect" in order to be loved was unconsciously pushing the love she sought away. As a single mother, she often felt alone with no one to talk to and she wanted to manifest a healthy relationship with a man who had his life together. Natalie longed to feel truly seen and heard by a man who valued her regardless of her external achievements. Her particular experience reminds me of this famous quote from best-selling author Marianne Williamson:

"Our deepest fear is not that we are inadequate. Our deepest fear is that we are powerful beyond measure. It is our light, not our darkness that most frightens us. We ask ourselves, 'Who am I to be brilliant, gorgeous, talented, fabulous?' Actually, who are you not to be? You are a child of God. Your playing small does not serve the world. There is nothing enlightened about shrinking so that other people won't feel insecure around you. We are all meant to shine, as children do. We were born to make manifest the glory of God that is within us. It's not just in some of us; it's in everyone. And as we let our own light shine, we unconsciously give other people permission to do the same. As we are liberated from our own fear, our presence automatically liberates others."

Once we were able to bring a conscious awareness into her patterns of self-sabotage, she was able to heal and write a new story. After our work together, Natalie feels more confident and comfortable in her own skin. She no longer seeks external validation, but rather values her own thoughts and opinions. She is setting healthy boundaries, honoring her needs, and respecting herself more fully. Natalie has created a deeper relationship with herself and experienced an amazing self-love transformation. In our work together, she learned the power of positive self-talk and showing herself compassion. She is less concerned with being "perfect" and more interested in being who she truly is. Natalie also stopped attracting toxic relationships because she is no longer willing to settle for less than what she deserves. She is currently involved with a gentleman who is kind, respectful, and sees the real Natalie. She can be herself around him and she does not feel that she has to pretend to be something she isn't in order to be worthy of love. It has been almost 2 years and they both care deeply for one another. Once she began to accept and love herself, it was easier to call in a healthy and fulfilling relationship. Natalie is now courageously putting her work out there and no longer feels the need to hide or dim her light. She is shining bright!

As Natalie's story so perfectly demonstrates, once we stop permitting others to define our worth, we take our power back and connect to our inner worthiness. When our self-worth is tied up in external things, it is easy to lose sight of who we are and our limitless value. In reality, what determines true worthiness is our inner essence and the spiritual qualities we possess such as kindness, compassion, integrity, generosity, etc. The goal is to make your self-worth an impenetrable fortress which no one or thing can invade or destroy. Your worth is like the sun which is always there even when the clouds (limiting beliefs) are blocking it. Here are 10 suggestions to help you tap into your inherent worth:

10 Self-Worth Tips:

1. Live with intention and purpose
2. Seek to understand your true self
3. Stop worrying what others think
4. Stand firm in the truth of who you are
5. Make a list of what doesn't define your worth
6. Develop and cultivate your virtues
7. Connect with a higher power (ex. God, the Universe, etc.)
8. Avoid people who undermine your integrity and worth
9. Walk away from unhealthy situations
10. Spend time with people who make you feel seen and heard

Knowing your worth looks like:

- Graciously accepting compliments
- Valuing your personal beliefs
- Not settling for less than what you deserve
- Expecting love and respect in all of your relationships
- Speaking your truth and communicating assertively
- Saying "no" without second-guessing yourself or feeling bad
- Releasing the need to constantly apologize
- Letting go of self-sabotaging behaviors
- Respecting and honoring your body
- Setting healthy boundaries with yourself and others

Activity #1:

Assertiveness Role Play

Instructions: Write down how you would respond to the following situations in a self-assured and assertive manner. Remember to speak calmly and firmly while communicating your wants and needs:

- Scenario #1: Your friend is always more than 15 minutes late for lunch and you have to wait for them which puts you behind schedule
- Scenario #2: You are dating someone new and their constant touching without your consent makes you feel uncomfortable
- Scenario #3: Your coworker asks you to cover for them but you already made important plans
- Scenario #4: Your neighbor plays their loud music at 1am and you need to get up early for work the next day

Activity #2:

Boundaries Exploration

Reflect on your personal boundaries and answer the following questions:

1. What boundaries are important to me?
2. Are my boundaries typically porous, rigid, or healthy? Why?
3. In what ways can I establish healthier boundaries with myself?
4. Who do I struggle setting boundaries with?
5. How can I more effectively communicate and maintain my boundaries with others?

Activity #3:

Self-Worth Sentence Frames

<u>Instructions:</u> For each of the following sentences, fill in the blank spaces below:

1. I'm secretly good at_____
2. One of my favorite things about myself is_____
3. I am so proud of myself for_____
4. I am exceptionally good at_____
5. _____does not define me.
6. I enjoy helping others with_____.
7. _____is one of the kindest things I've ever done for someone else.

8. My ability to _____ is improving.

9. _____ is what makes me special.

10. _____ is something I want to cultivate more of in my life.

Step 7

Strengthen Your Confidence (Self-Confidence)

"Self-confidence is a superpower. Once you start believing in yourself, magic starts happening" -Anonymous

In my all-time favorite movie, *The Holiday* starring Kate Winslet, Cameron Diaz, Jude Law, and Jack Black, there is a scene where one of the main characters, Iris, is struggling with her confidence and her wise mentor, Arthur, has this to say: *"Iris, in the movies we have leading ladies and we have the best friend. You, I can tell, are a leading lady, but for some reason, you're behaving like the best friend."* We've all been there. Self-confidence is trusting and believing in ourselves, our abilities, and our capabilities. When we are lacking confidence, we are essentially hiding our light whilst not allowing others to see the *real* us. It may be because we have been hurt in the past, fear rejection, or want to escape judgement. This quote from Aristotle sums it up quite nicely: *"To avoid criticism, do nothing, say nothing, and be nothing."* Mic drop. You are here at this particular moment in history to express your authenticity and become who you were meant to be.

This chapter is infused with tools and tips to help you show up as the most confident and empowered version of yourself. True self-confidence means releasing self-doubt, banishing imposter syndrome, trusting yourself, and feeling good in your skin. The cure to self-doubt is self-belief (or self-efficacy) which is the confidence in one's abilities to reach their goals. In this chapter, we will discuss how to let go of self-doubt, break free of imposter syndrome, and learn to trust ourselves more. We will also explore the power of authenticity, divine feminine energy, and main character energy in relation to building our confidence. Lastly, we will analyze psychologist Dr. Julian Rotter's Locus of Control with regards to feeling in control and empowered in our lives.

Self-doubt is the kryptonite of true confidence and empowerment. It weakens our efforts, causes uncertainty, and makes us question ourselves and our capabilities. Self-doubt keeps us fearfully paralyzed in our comfort zones, terrified of judgement or failure. When we are doubting ourselves, our inner critic is running the show which prevents growth and expansion. We are also more likely to experience self-criticism and personal judgement when our doubts take over. Ironically, self-doubt is a self-fulfilling prophecy which can lead to anxiety, depression, insecurities, procrastination, lack of motivation, indecisiveness, and a poor self-image. Doubting or being hard on ourselves is never the path toward self-improvement. Everyone has experienced self-doubt at one point in their lives, but the important thing is to recognize it when it shows up and take appropriate action. Since our self-doubts have become learned habits, we can unlearn them as well. Below are 10 ways to banish self-doubt for good:

10 Ways to Overcome Self-Doubt:

1. Challenge negative or self-defeating beliefs
2. Replace with encouraging and supportive thoughts
3. Quit the comparison game

4. Stop seeking external approval or validation
5. Don't take anything personally
6. Stop making assumptions
7. View setbacks as temporary
8. Remember you are your toughest critic
9. Be your own cheerleader
10. Reflect on your past achievements

Imposter Syndrome

What I know

What I think other people know

→

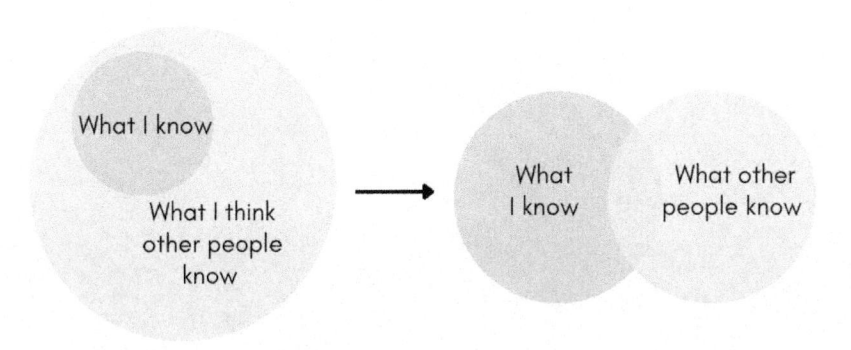

What I know

What other people know

Dr. Pauline Clance & Dr. Suzanne Imes (1978)

Recognizing that you are capable as well as learning to believe and trust in yourself are vital aspects of self-love, however imposter syndrome can get in the way. Coined in the 1970's by clinical psychologists Dr. Pauline Clance and Dr. Suzanne Imes, imposter syndrome is all too common among women who are socially conditioned to doubt and question themselves and who may refuse to take credit for their contributions. Here's an example: have you ever noticed how some women say, "I think" before making a statement as opposed to their male counterparts who are generally more decisive and self-assured? I myself have struggled with not feeling good enough as well as my clients. Imposter syndrome is the psychological belief that someone is inherently inadequate or a "fraud." Common symptoms include self-doubt, insecurities, and fear of failure. If you are struggling with imposter syndrome, here are 10 simple ways to help kick it to the curb:

10 Ways to Stop Imposter Syndrome:

1. Be aware of your triggers
2. Stop comparing yourself to others
3. Embrace "failure" and making mistakes
4. Be willing to ask for help
5. Let go of perfectionism
6. Be kind to yourself
7. Focus on your capabilities
8. Visualize success
9. Accept credit for your accomplishments
10. Celebrate your victories

Imposter Syndrome Cycle

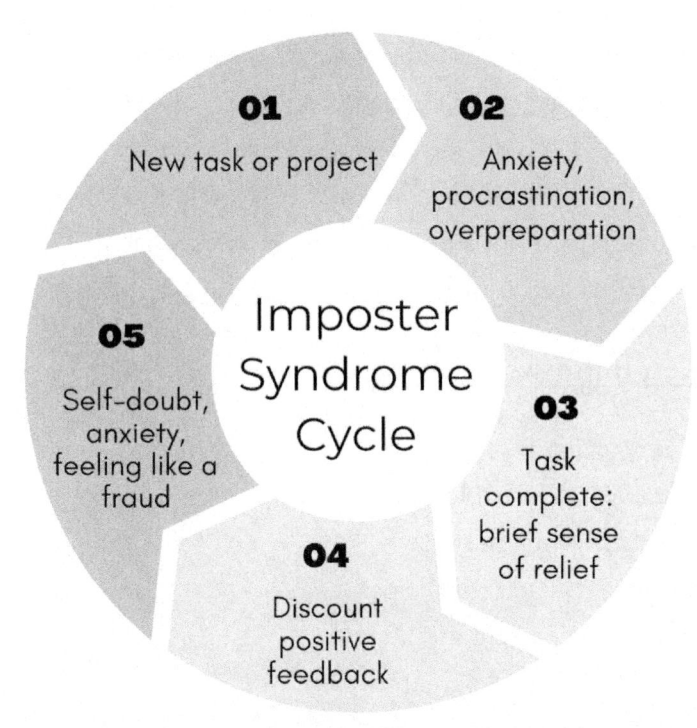

- **01** New task or project
- **02** Anxiety, procrastination, overpreparation
- **03** Task complete: brief sense of relief
- **04** Discount positive feedback
- **05** Self-doubt, anxiety, feeling like a fraud

Dr. Pauline Clance & Dr. Suzanne Imes (1978)

Self-trust is another essential element in the self-love formula. Our ability to trust ourselves is directly related to our level of confidence. Think about it: if someone does not have faith in themself to make the right decisions, they are typically suffering from a serious lack of confidence and clarity. Self-trust involves honoring and validating our thoughts, opinions, and feelings. On my self-love journey, learning to trust myself was particularly difficult as I had previously pushed myself to the point of panic or exhaustion. Rebuilding my relationship with myself included trusting my gut, setting reasonable goals, and not worrying what others thought in the process. Since I was loving myself more, I recognized that I had my best interest in mind and I would make decisions that would benefit my life. I recognized that worrying and overthinking were not serving me and that I was capable of steering my life in the right direction. Trusting ourselves does not mean that we need to have all of the answers or that we won't make mistakes along the way. Instead, it means that we trust ourselves enough to handle whatever happens and that we will show ourselves grace and compassion regardless of the outcome. Self-trust is about living in the present moment and not letting the past keep us stuck or the future make us fearful. Here are 10 simple tips to strengthen your self-trust:

10 Tips to Improve Self-Trust:

1. Start small
2. Establish reasonable goals
3. Check in with yourself
4. Forgive yourself for the past
5. Stay in the present moment
6. Hold yourself accountable
7. Commit to your well-being
8. Provide space to process your emotions
9. Spend time with trustworthy people
10. Release habits/routines that weaken your self-trust

Now let's take a look at the importance of authenticity which is a true marker of self-confidence and empowerment. When we show up as our authentic self, we are genuine, real, and sincere. Authentic individuals are honest and truthful with themselves and others. They do not feel the need to put on airs or portray themselves in a certain way to be accepted or receive approval. The first step is to take off the mask and be vulnerable with those you trust. The people who truly love you will want to discover who you are and what matters to you. Interestingly enough, when we stop trying to be something that we are not, we are more likely to attract meaningful and fulfilling relationships. Additionally, we are also able to build a lasting and purposeful relationship with ourselves. These are 10 ways to help you show up more authentically in your life:

10 Authenticity Tips:

1. Reevaluate your core beliefs
2. Live in alignment with your values
3. Embrace what makes you different
4. Open up to others
5. Be honest and truthful
6. Release how other people respond
7. Learn to laugh at yourself
8. Don't take yourself too seriously
9. Show yourself gratitude and appreciation
10. Surround yourself with loving people

One way to tap into your inner confidence is to connect with the divine feminine energy within you. Divine feminine energy is the goddess inside of you who is waiting to emerge. She is receptive, open, gentle, graceful, creative, powerful, and so much more. She is also the epitome of love and radiates compassion and empathy toward others. The divine feminine is spontaneous and surrenders to the present moment. Awakening this energy is not about biology or reproductive parts, but rather connecting to the female spirit. Here are 10 tips to ignite your divine feminine energy:

10 Divine Feminine Energy Tips:

1. Move your body

Dancing and sensual movement release blocked energy and are a wonderful expression of the divine feminine. I have a music playlist called, "Bossbabe" that always leaves me feeling empowered and ready to take on the world!

2. *Indulge your senses*

Lavish yourself with delicious foods and truly savor every bite. Use essential oils in a relaxing bath to pamper your inner goddess or treat yourself to a self-care day at home

3. *Spend time in nature*

Connecting with Mother Earth is an excellent way to embrace the sacred feminine within you. Walk barefoot in the dirt, swim in a lake or ocean, or relax near a fire pit

4. *Listen to your intuition*

Honor your sensitivities and trust your gut instincts. If something feels off, it usually is. Your internal navigation will show you the way

5. *Feel your emotions*

Acknowledge your emotions and let them be without resistance. Hold space for whatever you are feeling without identification or judgement. This will permit them to pass sooner

6. *Interpret your dreams*

Reflect on memorable or reoccurring dreams you have and contemplate their significance and meaning related to your life Dreams are a portal into our inner world and they may provide a message you need to hear

7. *Reclaim your power*

Never allow yourself to be controlled, manipulated, or oppressed. You are a force of nature and should not have to submit to anyone

8. *Connect with like-minded women*

We are stronger together. I could not do what I do without my amazing community of women who inspire and support one another. Embrace and surround yourself with your sisters and lift each other up!

9. *Be open to receiving*

When we are too much in our masculine energy, it can be more difficult to receive the infinite abundance and blessings that life has to offer. If someone gives you a compliment, accept it! Keep in mind that you don't have to try so hard because we can never lose what is meant for us

10. *Think like a goddess*

Would a goddess spend her weekend waiting for a guy to text her or would she get out there and live her best life? When making a decision ask yourself: *what would a goddess do?*

As previously mentioned, you are the main character of your story and can always rewrite the script. If you are not satisfied with how things are going, pick up a pen and make a change. Main character energy is not about being selfish, entitled, or treating others as your "supporting cast," but rather becoming your best self and living an intentionally purpose-filled life. It is showing up as the protagonist of your story and feeling confident to take on whatever life has to offer. Main character energy lets life happen for you rather than to you. Tapping into the main character within you will allow you to shine like the bright star you are. Acting like the leading lady of your story is a serious confidence booster and reminds you that you are in control of your life. You are so much more powerful and capable than you may have been led to realize. Here are 10 tips for harnessing main character energy:

10 Main Character Energy Tips:

1. Create a personal soundtrack
2. Prioritize your goals
3. Forge your own path
4. Act with purpose
5. Stop caring what people think
6. Enjoy your alone time
7. Remember your power
8. Add enthusiasm to everyday tasks
9. Be true to yourself
10. Explore the world

Individuals who are the main character of their story typically have an internal rather than an external locus of control. Developed by psychologist Dr. Julian Rotter, locus of control refers to the amount of power an individual believes they have over themselves and their life. Those who possess an external locus of control are more likely to blame outside forces for their misfortunes, as opposed to those with an internal locus of control who believe that they are the ones in charge of their lives. Studies show that those who have an internal locus of control are more independent and less swayed by the opinions of others. The goal is to develop an internal locus of control so that we believe in ourselves and our capabilities which will help strengthen our confidence. You got this!

Locus of Control

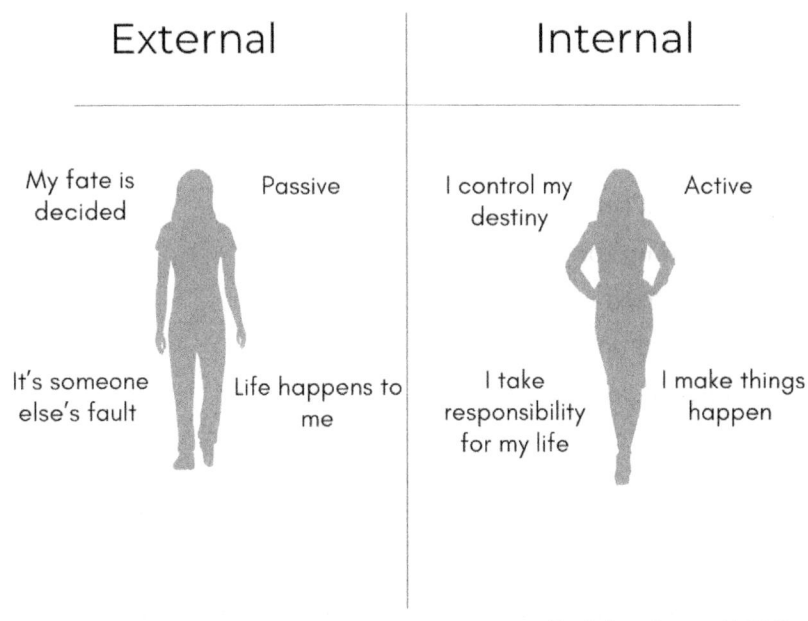

External	Internal
My fate is decided	I control my destiny
Passive	Active
It's someone else's fault	I take responsibility for my life
Life happens to me	I make things happen

Dr. Julian Rotter (1954)

Strengthening your confidence looks like:

- Owning your power
- Taking responsibility for your life
- Being open to new challenges
- Believing in yourself and your capabilities
- Releasing self-doubt
- Focusing on the positive
- Taking a social media break
- Refusing to dim your light for anyone
- Taking credit for your accomplishments

from loved ones or professionals. Self-care is also not a "cure" for mental health issues or personal struggles. It is more than a "quick fix" or putting a band-aid over our exhaustion. Self-care is also not "one-size-fits-all" and is unique to each individual. What is considered self-care to one person might be stressful to another. Keep in mind that self-care does not have to be a time-consuming or elaborate routine.

Self-Care

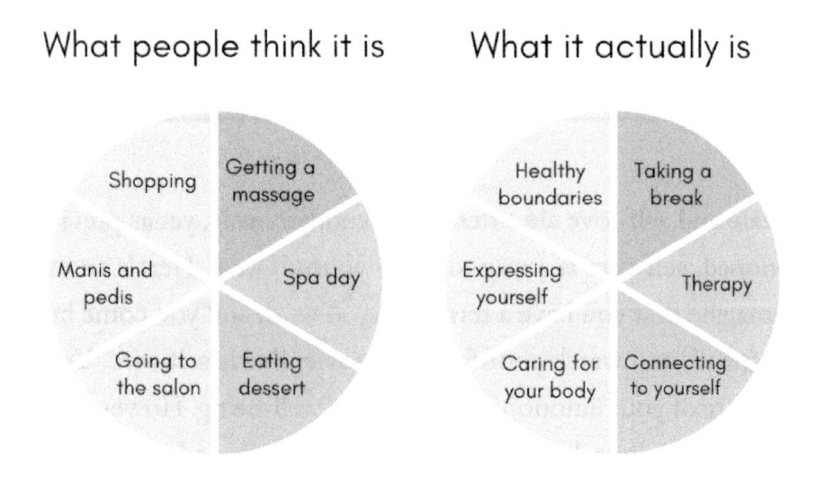

What people think it is

- Shopping
- Getting a massage
- Manis and pedis
- Spa day
- Going to the salon
- Eating dessert

What it actually is

- Healthy boundaries
- Taking a break
- Expressing yourself
- Therapy
- Caring for your body
- Connecting to yourself

In reality, self-care can be saying "no," setting healthy boundaries, and standing up for ourselves. Burnout can occur from people-pleasing or lack of boundaries. When we establish healthy boundaries from the beginning, we are treating the issue and not just the symptoms. Self-care is also managing stress, maintaining our emotional well-being, and caring for our mental health. It can be as simple as reaching out and connecting with a trusted friend. Caring for ourselves means recognizing when we could use extra support. Self-care includes coping strategies which can help when we are struggling or are feeling overwhelmed.

In this chapter, we will cover the role of coping skills, nurturing ourselves, and the 5 love languages as they relate to self-care. We will also analyze the 8 types of self-care, which includes spiritual self-care. Spiritual self-care is particularly helpful as it feeds your soul while renewing your energy. It reconnects you to your higher self and The Universe. It is uplifting, inspiring, and restorative. Holistic self-care includes our mind, body and spirit. This allows us to raise our frequency and in turn attract high vibe people, circumstances, and experiences. Lastly, there is a short section dedicated to empath self-care.

Developing healthy coping skills when life gets challenging is an essential aspect of self-care. Coping skills are ways to handle uncomfortable emotions or difficult situations as they arise. Tuning in and giving ourselves what we need in any given moment is especially important so that we know how to tend to and comfort ourselves. Depending on the specific scenario, self-care can be a variety of different things. One day it may be hiding under the covers, yet the next morning it might be getting out in the sunshine. Every situation is unique and it is important to listen to your intuition and internal guidance. Here are 8 major coping strategies:

8 Coping Skills:

1. *Self-soothing*-ways to comfort and nurture yourself (ex. deep breathing, weighted blanket, etc.).
2. *Relaxation*-activities that help you loosen up and unwind (ex. progressive muscle relaxation, calming app, etc.).

3. *Tension release*-allows you to process uncomfortable or painful feelings (ex. letting yourself cry, screaming in a pillow, dancing, moving your body, etc.).
4. *Mindfulness*-tools for centering yourself in the present moment (ex. 5-4-3-2-1 technique, guided meditation, cuddling with a pet, etc.).
5. *Distraction*-ways to refocus your mind (ex. reading, listening to music, watching TV/movies, etc.).
6. *Cognitive reframing*-challenging negative thoughts and replacing them with more realistic beliefs (ex. questioning your inner critic, not believing everything you think, etc.).
7. *Building resilience*-the ability to adapt and recover after facing adversity (ex. being flexible, using problem solving skills, focusing on a goal, etc.).
8. *Asking for help*-reaching out to others for support (ex. calling a friend, therapy, joining a support group, etc.).

Now we will explore how nurturing ourselves is a prime example of self-care. Self-nurturing is the act of nourishing and caring for ourselves. This means that we engage in activities which replenish our energy and feed our soul. Nurturing ourselves allows us to connect with the truth of who we are and show up as the highest version of ourselves. We address our needs and prioritize our physical, mental, and emotional well-being. Self-nurturing can also be used as a preventative measure to avoid exhaustion or burnout. When we nourish ourselves, we feel energized, strong, and capable to handle whatever life throws our way. Here are 10 ideas to help you nurture yourself more:

10 Self-Nurturing Ideas:

1. Create a cozy space
2. Cuddle with a pet or loved one

3. Spend time in nature
4. Learn when to slow down
5. Conserve your energy
6. Practice moderation
7. Engage in a relaxing hobby
8. Prioritize your hopes and dreams
9. Take a vacation or staycation
10. Be more content with your life

In the #1 New York Times bestselling book, *The 5 Love Languages: The Secret to Love that Lasts,* author Dr. Gary Chapman outlines the 5 ways of giving and receiving love in relationships, which can also be used to show ourselves love and care as well. Take the Self-Love Quiz: https://findingjulianne.com/self-love-language-quiz/

Depending on your unique love language, here are a few suggestions to practice self-care:

<u>Words of Affirmation:</u>

- Eliminate negative thinking
- Positive self-talk
- Incorporate affirmations or mantras
- Compliment yourself
- Start a gratitude journal

<u>Physical Touch:</u>

- Massage
- Yoga
- Body scrub/loofah
- Jade roller
- Hot bath/cool shower

Acts of Service:

- Clean your space
- Meal prep
- Get organized
- Pay off any debt
- Order takeout/delivery

Gifts:

- Do your hair/nails
- Buy something fancy
- Invest in yourself
- Try a new hobby/class
- Take yourself on a date

Quality Time:

- Journal
- Read
- Pray/meditate
- Create something
- Set healthy boundaries

Protecting your energy is an essential element of self-care. Prioritizing what is important in your life will help you live in alignment with your values. Only say "yes" to things that feel intuitively right to you. People may be disappointed and that's okay because we cannot make everyone happy. Would you want someone to do something that they did not want to do? I didn't think so! The people who truly care and love you will respect your needs. Caring for ourselves can be truly transformative as demonstrated in the following client story:

Natalie's Story Part 2

"I'm always taking on too much which leaves me depleted and exhausted," Natalie said.

As a recovering people-pleaser and perfectionist, this was a common theme in Natalie's life. Natalie was no stranger to feeling tired and burnt out. With her numerous commitments and responsibilities, caring for herself was often the last thing on her mind. Natalie works full-time, has two teenage sons, is a dedicated member of her faith, and is extremely involved in her community which often leaves little time for herself. She was always concerned with everyone else's happiness and her own well-being took a backseat. The irony was that the more she put on her plate, the less effective she felt in her work. In our sessions together, Natalie released old patterns and ways of thinking which were no longer serving her. She realized that she did not need to keep a non-stop itinerary to prove her worth because she was already enough. Natalie and I created a self-care schedule and I gave her a self-care planner which held her accountable for making herself a priority. Like many recovering perfectionists, Natalie is a type-A personality so feeling organized and having a self-care checklist benefited her immensely.

Perhaps the greatest breakthrough that she experienced was that she finally believed that she was just as deserving of her time and energy as anyone else. Natalie is still a busy woman, but during our time together she started taking better care of herself and addressing her needs more. The last time we spoke, she was making time for her artistic and creative pursuits and engaging in activities that connected her to her true self. After completing the program, Natalie told me that she was, *"so happy she took the plunge"* and now she is better able to achieve balance in her life.

As Natalie's story attests, setting aside time for self-care can be quite challenging in our busy lives. I recommend writing it in a planner or setting a phone reminder to schedule self-care. Self-care can become a habit and part of your daily routine. It can be as simple as setting aside 30 minutes each day to do something you enjoy. Remember that you are just as deserving of your time, energy and attention as anyone else so make yourself a priority. When we fill up our own cup first, we have more to offer others. Be sure to tailor your self-care toward your needs and remove any pressure or expectations. Self-care is meant to reduce stress and make you feel better and rejuvenated. Taking care of ourselves is not a luxury, it is a necessity.

Next, let's consider the eight types of self-care and their practical application:

8 Types of Self-Care:

1. *Physical*-taking care of your physical health and well-being (ex. sleep, healthy eating, exercise, fresh air, etc.).
2. *Emotional*-caring for your emotional needs with kindness and compassion (ex. positive reassurance, journaling, managing stress, etc.).
3. *Social*-connecting and building relationships with others (ex. friends, boundaries, social network, etc.).
4. *Spiritual*-connecting to your spiritual or religious beliefs (ex. alone time, meditation, prayer, time in nature, etc.).
5. *Personal*-taking time for what you love and enjoy (ex. hobbies, goals, etc.).
6. *Environmental*-keeping a clean, safe and functional living space (ex. regular cleaning, decluttering, comfy spaces, etc.).
7. *Financial*-maintaining financial responsibilities and obligations (ex. paying bills, budgeting, saving, etc.).

8. *Occupational*-addressing your needs related to work, school, or caregiving (ex. communicating your needs, taking breaks, time management, etc.).

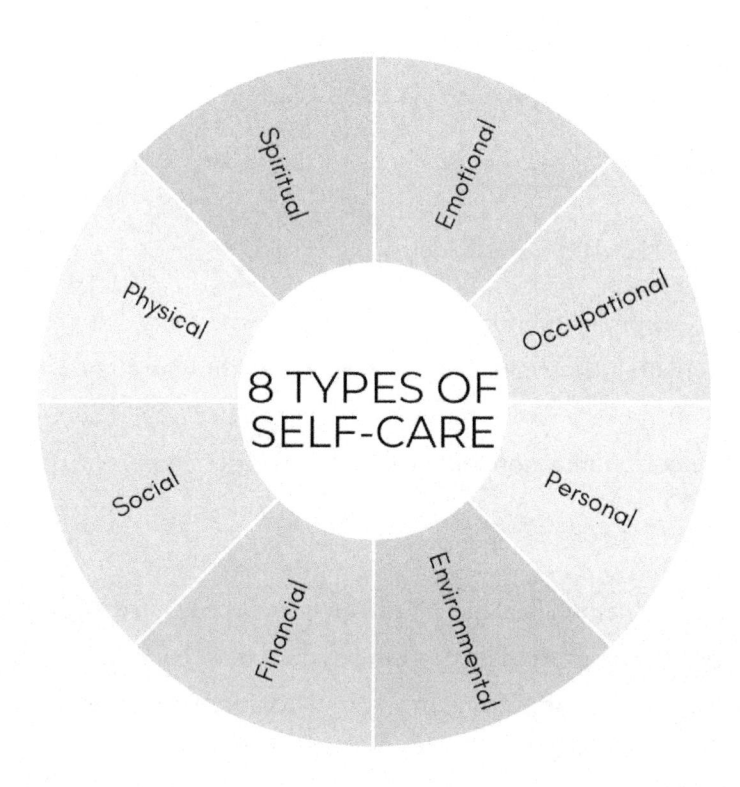

8 TYPES OF SELF-CARE

- Spiritual
- Emotional
- Physical
- Occupational
- Social
- Personal
- Financial
- Environmental

Since myself and the majority of my clients are empaths, I wanted to include a short section highlighting empath self-care. An empath is a highly sensitive individual who easily takes on the emotional energy of others. These individuals are extremely thoughtful, caring, and compassionate. Empaths can often sense what another person is feeling or experiencing without the person explicitly expressing their emotions. Given that empaths are incredibly sensitive, they may struggle with anxiety, depression, fatigue, exhaustion, boundary issues, overthinking, etc. Therefore, it is vital that an empath's self-care ritual is calming, nourishing, and restorative. If you are an empath, these essential tools can help protect your energy and harness your power. If you are not an empath, you still may find these suggestions useful.

Are you an empath? Take the quiz!
https://drjudithorloff.com/quizzes/empath-self-assessment-test/

5 Empath Self-Care Tips:

1. Block or Limit Energy Vampires

Energy vampires are individuals who suck your energy dry and provide you with little or nothing in return. Empaths tend to be narcissist magnets if they aren't diligently guarding their energy. This is where assertive communication and healthy boundaries are essential

2. Ground Yourself

Empaths are natural healers and caregivers who take on a lot of energy and may require grounding. Grounding brings us back to the present moment when we are feeling overstimulated or overwhelmed. Examples include: splashing cool water on your face, smelling essential oils, deep breathing, etc.

3. Practice Energetic Cleansing

Energetic cleansing or energetic clearing pushes out old energy which creates space for higher vibrations. Examples include: smudging, yoga, meditation, etc. Smudging involves burning sacred herbs to attract positive energy. One of my favorite ways to release negative energy is to take an empath bath (ingredients: 1 cup Epsom salt, ½ cup baking soda, ½ cup pink Himalayan Sea salt, and essential oils) (Source: *The Empath's Workbook*, 2020)

4. *Prioritize Alone Time*

Due to their vivid imaginations, empaths require time away from the hustle and bustle of society to explore their inner world. Empaths are often highly creative and spending time in a quiet space can allow them to discover their artistic pursuits. Engaging in sacred alone time offers empaths a sense of peace and balance in their lives. This can also be a place of refuge to recharge their energy and connect with their higher self. Spending time in nature or with animals is indispensable for empaths

5. *Trust Your Intuition*

Empaths are often blessed with a strong intuition which is a spiritual gift that can be used to serve themselves and others. It is important to always validate your feelings and trust your inner knowing. You are a natural manifester so follow your intuitive nudges

Incorporating self-care looks like:

- Developing coping skills
- Engaging in uplifting activities
- Caring for your body, mind, & spirit
- Making time for yourself
- Identifying your top priorities
- Establishing comforting routines
- Limiting screen time
- Organizing and decluttering your life
- Saying "no" and not over-committing
- Asking for what you need

Activity #1:

8 Types of Self-Care

<u>Instructions</u>: For each of the 8 forms of self-care, write down how you can incorporate more of it into your life:

1. Physical
2. Emotional
3. Social
4. Spiritual
5. Personal
6. Environmental
7. Financial
8. Occupational

Activity #2:

Self-Care Cup

<u>Instructions</u>: This activity provides the opportunity to assess and reflect on the people, places, and things that drain you and the ones that pour into your cup:

1. Write 5 signs that you are feeling exhausted or overwhelmed
2. Write 5 things that empty your cup
3. Write 5 things that fill your cup
4. Write 3 people who support you
5. Write 3 places that calm you

Activity #3:

Take Yourself on a Date

<u>Instructions</u>: Make a list of your favorite activities and plan to take yourself on a "me date." Consider where you will go and what you will be doing

Here are a few ideas:

1. Buy yourself flowers
2. Dinner and a movie
3. Explore the city
4. Staycation
5. Walk around the park
6. Do something creative
7. Take a solo trip
8. Hang out in a café
9. Go to the zoo
10. Take a class

Step 9

Keep Growing
(Self-Growth)

"There is only one corner of the universe that you can be sure of improving and it is yourself" –Aldous Huxley

The practice of self-love is quite similar to tending a garden. It requires continued attention to cultivate and grow the beauty within. An important aspect of self-love is working toward the things we are passionate about and setting new goals. Although it is essential to accept wherever we are on our personal journey, we are also constantly evolving into a higher version of ourselves. Self-growth is a continual state of broadening and improving ourselves. Self-improvement paves the way in the present for our future selves. Engaging in self-growth not only strengths our relationship with ourselves, it also helps us develop our unique abilities and skills. Self-development allows us to remove the layers obscuring our true selves from fully showing up in the world. Improving ourselves is a life-long process that is filled with constant changes.

In this chapter, we will compare the difference between a fixed mindset versus a growth mindset as well as tips on how to cultivate a growth mindset. We will also cover Gardner's Theory of Multiple

Intelligences and how discovering yours can make learning easier and more enjoyable. As well, we will consider the Johari Window which is a beneficial self-development tool that can strengthen our self-knowledge. Additionally, we will examine the role of self-leadership, self-reflection, and the 5 Stages of Change model which can be helpful when reaching your goals. Finally, we will review what it means to be a self-actualized person and the common characteristics they possess.

Before we can achieve our aspirations, it is important to become aware of our mindset as this will determine how we feel and the probability of our success. Psychologist Dr. Carol Dweck developed the concept of the fixed versus the growth mindset based on extensive study and research into the capacity of the human brain. Dweck's theory of neuroplasticity confirms that the brain continues to form new connections into adulthood, even if it has been damaged, which supports the concept of the growth mindset.

Those who possess a fixed mindset believe that skills, intelligence, and talents are natural and cannot be developed. A fixed mindset is full of limiting and self-defeating beliefs which hinder true progress. In this state of mind, the individual believes that they are not in control of their abilities and that some people can do things and others cannot. They typically avoid challenges and constructive feedback, strive for perfection, and become defensive when they make a mistake. With regards to the fixed mindset, failure is avoided at all costs, effort is seen as a waste of time since talents are innate, and giving up when things get hard is commonplace. These individuals are more likely to criticize themselves, judge others, and feel threatened by their success. A person with a fixed mindset is inclined to hide their "flaws" and not reach out to others for support. Ultimately, the fixed mindset is devoid of self-love and compassion because it constantly compares ourselves to others, keeps us stuck without the possibility for growth, and causes us to believe that we are not inherently enough.

On the other hand, the growth mindset unlocks the potential for our greatest hopes and dreams to become fully realized. Those who possess a growth mindset believe that they are capable of developing their intelligence, talents, and skills and are continually seeking to improve themselves. They view mistakes and failure as an opportunity for growth, are receptive to feedback, and accept setbacks as a part of the learning process. These individuals are willing to take on new challenges, keep going despite obstacles, and demonstrate sustained effort. A person with a growth mindset believes that they are in control of their abilities, are always advancing themselves, and seek out help and support from others. Those with a growth mindset practice self-compassion, encourage others on their journey, and view other's success as a source of inspiration and evidence for what is possible for them. Who wouldn't want to have such an outlook on life? Here are 10 ideas to help you foster a growth mindset and tap into the unlimited potential within you!

10 Ways to Develop a Growth Mindset:

1. Ask questions
2. Keep learning
3. Prioritize growth over speed
4. See challenges as opportunities
5. Don't give up too quickly
6. Keep moving toward your goals
7. Allow yourself to make mistakes
8. Be open to constructive criticism
9. View failure as feedback
10. Practice active reflection

According to Harvard psychologist Dr. Howard Gardner, people have different types of "intelligences" or ways of obtaining and learning new information. Becoming aware of your unique learning style(s) can help you recognize your natural strengths and support you on your path toward growth and self-development. It can also provide a deeper appreciation and understanding of your personality and character traits. Gardner's Multiple Intelligence Theory originally included eight types of intelligence, however in recent years, he added a ninth one. These intelligences are broken down into nine categories of perceiving the world and retaining knowledge. Keep in mind that you may identify with more than one intelligence and that is totally okay. Take the quiz below:

https://www.idrlabs.com/multiple-intelligences/test.php

9 Types of Intelligence:

1. *Visual-Spatial:* prefers images and pictures (ex. drawing, creating puzzles, watching TV/movies, etc.).
2. *Linguistic-Verbal:* uses words and language (ex. reading, writing, storytelling, etc.).
3. *Logical-Mathematical:* recognizes relationships, patterns, or trends (ex. analyzing problems, solving equations, reasoning, etc.).
4. *Bodily-Kinesthetic:* enjoys using the body and possesses a strong muscle memory (ex. playing sports, dancing, acting, etc.).
5. *Musical:* thinks in sounds and patterns; recognizes tone, melody, and rhythm (ex. playing an instrument, singing, composing, etc.).
6. *Interpersonal:* excellent at interacting and sensing the emotions of others (ex. working in a group, teaching, leading, etc.).

7. *Intrapersonal:* understands oneself, introspective, and self-aware (ex. working independently, journaling, self-reflecting, etc.).
8. *Naturalistic:* observes patterns and relationships in nature (ex. hiking, gardening, camping, etc.).
9. *Existential:* uses thought, intuition, and metacognition to understand the world (ex. deep conversations, volunteering, serving humanity, etc.).

An important aspect of self-improvement is continually developing our self-knowledge and identifying potential areas of growth. Created by psychologists Dr. Joseph Luft and Dr. Harrington Ingham, the Johari Window is an excellent resource used in self-development and leadership to give us a more comprehensive understanding of our ourselves and our potential blind spots. It can help us improve our communication skills, strengthen our relationships, and connect us to ourselves on a deeper level. Let's explore the 4 quadrants of the Johari Window as well as suggestions to support your growth:

The Johari Window:

1. Unknown-*(unknown to self; unknown to others)*

Information about yourself that is unknown to you and everyone else; includes information in the subconscious mind, hidden talents, and the future self (tip: engage in inner child healing and shadow work).

2. Blind-*(unknown to self; known to others)*

Information about yourself which is known to others yet you are unaware of (tip: be open to feedback from trusted individuals).

3. <u>Hidden</u>-*(known to self; unknown to others)*

Information about yourself that you are aware of, but others are not; can be a façade or mask (tip: disclose information when you feel comfortable).

4. <u>Open</u> -*(known to self; known to others)*

Information about yourself known to you and others; the public self (tip: continue to open up and share with trusted parties).

The Johari Window

Known to self   *Not known to self*

	Known to self	Not known to self
Known to others	**Open Self** — Information about yourself known to you and others	**Blind Self** — Information about yourself unknown to you but others know
Not known to others	**Hidden Self** — Information about yourself known to you but not others	**Unknown Self** — Information about yourself unknown to you and others

Dr. Joseph Luft & Dr. Harrington Ingham (1955)

Do you consider yourself a leader or a follower? Did you know it is possible to lead *yourself*? Coined by professor Dr. Charles Manz, self-leadership is the practice of knowing who you are, what your goals are, and how to reach your desired outcomes. Put simply, it is understanding who we are, what we do, and how we do it. Leading ourselves means being aware of our strengths, weaknesses, and untapped potential. Self-leadership calls us to motivate, inspire, and encourage ourselves toward growth and obtaining our goals. We are intentional about where we are going and the steps to take us there. Additionally, we are able to identify and understand gaps in our knowledge and possible areas of improvement. The Johari Window previously mentioned is an excellent resource for developing self-leadership. According to research, effective self-leaders possess 8 core competences or skills:

8 Core Self-Leadership Skills:

1. *Self-awareness and self-knowledge:* understanding who you are and how to self-regulate
2. *Identifying desired experiences:* clearly defining your goals and dreams
3. *Constructive thought and decision-making:* maintaining a positive attitude and practicing mindfulness
4. *Planning and goal setting:* breaking down goals into small achievable steps
5. *Optimizing motivation:* aligning your goals with your values to make the process more enticing and appealing
6. *Harnessing the ecosystem:* utilizing your environment to help you reach your goals (ex. connecting with others, asking for support, etc.).
7. *Amplifying our performance:* checking in and supporting yourself on your journey
8. *Embracing failure and cultivating grit:* viewing failure as an opportunity for growth and continuing on with your goals

Interested in harnessing your self-leadership abilities? Brilliant psychologist and personal friend, Dr. Maike Neuhaus offers several suggestions for embracing your inner leader and taking ownership of your life. Dr. Neuhaus specializes in self-leadership, so I am thrilled to be able to share some of her insights and wisdom from the research. Here are 15 tips to help you become the captain of your ship and direct yourself toward exactly where you want to be in your life:

15 Self-Leadership Tips:

1. Practice self-observation
2. Exude curiosity and humility
3. Clearly define your goals
4. Envision your desired outcome
5. Visualize yourself taking action
6. Build helpful habits
7. Develop a growth mindset
8. Adapt to change
9. Exercise self-discipline
10. Invest in yourself
11. Be proactive
12. Take calculated risks
13. Monitor your progress
14. Reward your efforts
15. Engage in self-reflection

Self-reflection involves examining our thoughts, feelings, and actions. Much like self-leadership, self-reflection encourages us to consider who we are, where we currently are, and where we are going. Research demonstrates that self-reflection is associated with greater personal development and higher life satisfaction. When we become aware of our unconscious reactions, it is a pivotal step toward self-reflection.

Reflecting on ourselves and our behaviors can promote healing and growth. It can also be helpful to examine our motives and why we do the things we do. Self-reflection can be as simple as taking account for our actions at the end of the day and their impact on ourselves and others. In order to fully support your ability to be introspective and examine yourself, here are 10 self-reflection tips:

10 Self-Reflection Tips:

1. Understand your thoughts and feelings
2. Label your emotions
3. Contemplate your motives and your "whys"
4. Look for observable habits or patterns
5. Respond instead of react
6. Be gentle with yourself
7. Don't ruminate, reflect
8. Be open to different perspectives
9. Set aside time for reflection
10. Journal what you learned each day

Is there an area of your life that you would like to change? If you are like most people, the answer is probably "yes," yet understanding how to go about making a sustainable shift is another question. Developed by psychologists Dr. James Prochaska and Dr. Carlo DiClemente, the 5 Stages of Change model offers insight into your current progress and the steps you need to take to reach your goal. These stages build upon each other and they demonstrate an individual's readiness for sustainable change. Following these steps will make lasting change more probable. Keep in mind that behavioral change is often not linear and facing obstacles and setbacks are common:

5 Stages of Change

1. <u>Precontemplation</u>-You are unaware, unwilling, or unable to make a change (next steps: raise awareness, consider what will happen if change does not occur, etc.).

2. <u>Contemplation</u>-You are open to the possibility of change but you are not sure how to go about it (next steps: make a pro/con list, understand potential challenges, etc.).

3. <u>Preparation</u>-You have committed to taking action and you are making the necessary plans (next steps: list your goals, write down each step, etc.).

4. <u>Action</u>-You are following through with your plan (next steps: reward your efforts, reach out for support, etc.).

5. <u>Maintenance</u>-You have reached your goal and you are maintaining your progress (next steps: develop coping strategies, learn how to prevent relapses, etc.).

Stages of Change

- Precontemplation **01**
- Contemplation **02**
- Preparation **03**
- Action **04**
- Maintenance **05**

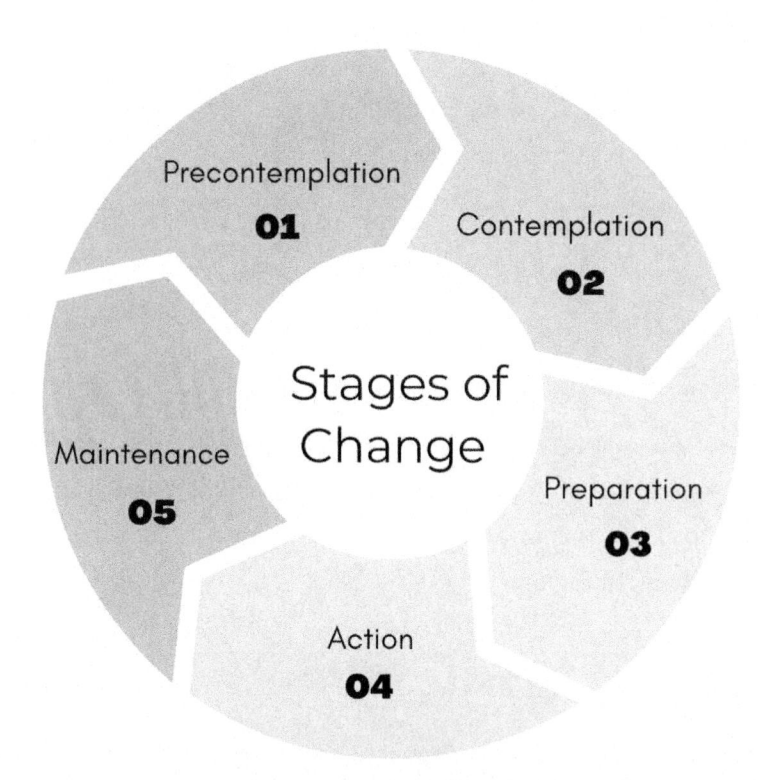

Dr. James Prochaska & Dr. Carlo DiClemente (1983)

To conclude this chapter, we will take a look at the role of self-actualization in relation to our personal growth. Self-actualization refers to one's personal potential becoming fully realized. Popularized by psychologist Dr. Abraham Maslow, self-actualization ranks highly on Maslow's Hierarchy of Needs. Originally, comprising five components, the expanded pyramid now includes eight essential stages for human development. When we are lacking an element, it can be difficult to completely understand ourselves and reach our highest potential. The pyramid is divided into two parts: deficiency needs and growth needs. The lower half represents deficiency needs (basic needs) and the top tier includes growth needs which stem from the desire to lead a fulfilling and inspired life.

Deficiency Needs:

1. *Physiological*-air, food, water, clothing, shelter, sleep
2. *Safety*-job stability and secure property
3. *Belonging and Love*-friendships, intimacy, relationships
4. *Esteem*-confidence, self-respect, self-worth

Growth Needs:

5. *Cognitive*-knowledge, meaning, self-awareness
6. *Aesthetic*-appreciation for beauty and balance
7. *Self-Actualization*-personal growth and fulfillment
8. *Transcendence*-spiritual or religious experiences, helping others, serving humanity

Maslow's Expanded Hiearchy of Needs

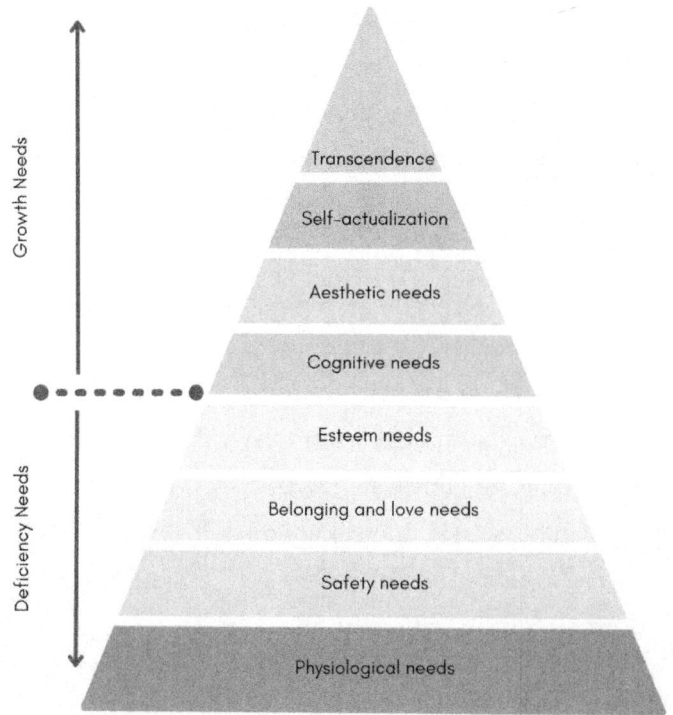

Growth Needs
Deficiency Needs

- Transcendence
- Self-actualization
- Aesthetic needs
- Cognitive needs
- Esteem needs
- Belonging and love needs
- Safety needs
- Physiological needs

Dr. Abraham Maslow (1970)

The interesting thing is that motivation decreases once our deficiency needs are met, yet when our growth needs are satisfied, we become more driven and motivated. Dr. Maslow notes that we can move up the ladder even if our deficiency needs are not completely met, it just makes progress easier when our lower needs are already satisfied. We may even move up and down the hierarchy which is completely normal, as growth is not always linear. Self-actualization is a process and not a specific destination we eventually reach. It is continually making our personal development a priority and accepting ourselves regardless of our stage along the journey. Let's take a look at Dr. Maslow's character traits of a self-actualized person:

Maslow's 15 Characteristics of Self-Actualized People:

1. Accept themselves and others
2. Keen sense of reality and can tolerate uncertainty
3. Able to view life objectively
4. Ability to fix problems without focusing on themselves
5. Healthy sense of humor that's not at the expense of others
6. Need for privacy and comfortable being alone
7. Democratic, fair, and non-discriminating of others
8. Non-conformist or unconventional
9. Establishes deep and meaningful relationships
10. Independently investigates the truth
11. Interested in everything, even ordinary things
12. Strong moral and ethical standards
13. Spontaneous, natural, and true to oneself
14. Creative, inventive, and original
15. Concerned for the welfare of humanity

Keep growing looks like:

- Staying open and curious
- Learning new things
- Developing a growth mindset
- Adapting to change
- Becoming more consistent
- Cultivating new skills
- Creating a vision board
- Setting tangible goals
- Rewarding your efforts, not the outcome
- Reflecting on your life

Activity #1:

Wheel of Life

Instructions: Draw a circle and divide it into 8 equal parts. Next, label each section using the categories below along with a number between 1-10 (10=highest) based on how satisfied you are with this area of your life. Lastly, write down your top 3 goals for each topic:

1. Personal growth
2. Work/career
3. Family/relationships
4. Money/finances
5. Health and well-being
6. Home environment
7. Fun and leisure
8. Faith/spirituality/life purpose

Activity #2:

My Vision Board

What you'll need:

- journal or poster board
- magazines
- scissors
- glue or tape
- pen or pencil
- colored pencils or markers
- (optional) stickers, glitter, lace, ribbon, craft supplies, etc.

Instructions: An excellent tool to manifest our dreams is to create a vision board. First, make a list of your goals, hopes, and dreams. Then select words and images that capture the direction you want your life to move toward. Be sure to choose images that resonate with you and make your heart soar. Cut out pictures that are aligned with your vision and paste them on the board. Doodle or write down words or phrases that correspond with your inspired plan. The trick is to truly *believe* that what is on the board is on its way to you. *Note: if you do not have access to the following materials, feel free to make a digital vision board on the Pinterest or Canva app.*

Activity #3:

Growth Mindset

Instructions: Select an area of your life that you want to grow in and answer the following questions:

1. What does a growth mindset look like?
2. In what areas of your life are you staying within your comfort zone?
3. How would you like to grow?
4. How have you already grown in this area?
5. What experiences or events could help you to grow?
6. Who could support your growth?
7. What is one action step you can take toward expansion?

Step 10

Love the World
(Self and Others)

"Not only do self-love and love of others go hand in hand but ultimately they are indistinguishable" -M. Scott Peck

So far in our time together, we have covered the path toward self-discovery, how to develop self-awareness, and how to accept yourself more fully. We have also explored the importance of practicing self-compassion, healing and releasing the past, recognizing your inherent worth, and building self-confidence on your self-love journey. Lastly, we reviewed the role of self-care and self-growth in maintaining your overall health and well-being. The final step of self-love is to become the embodiment of *love*. The goal is that now you have filled up your cup enough so that it may overflow to others. True self-love ripples out into the world and touches everyone you meet. After working together, my former client Seviana told me, *"now I talk to myself like a best friend."* She is inspiring those around her and is a self-love role model for her friends and family. Seviana uplifts and empowers her loved ones with positive and encouraging messages of kindness. Her story demonstrates that self-love is contagious, spreading light and hope to everyone it reaches.

In this final chapter, we will explore your unique life purpose, developing your talents and gifts to serve humanity, and the importance of connecting deeply with a Higher Power. I will refer to this Higher Power as God or The Universe but feel free to substitute any term you are comfortable with. If you have yet to discover your purpose, I will reveal the 5-step process I share with my clients in finding their mission on earth. We will also break down The Golden Rule, the 12 Universal Laws, and the 12 Laws of Karma and how understanding them can contribute to a purposeful and fulfilling life. The more you love and cherish yourself and others, the higher your vibration and the greater love and abundance you will attract. No matter how things are working out, trust the journey and believe that you are being led to exactly where you are meant to be.

Finding your purpose provides you with a deeper appreciation for the unique abilities, faculties, and talents which only you have to share with the world. Loving ourselves is directly connected to our relationships with others because when we show ourselves love and compassion and remember our common humanity, we find a greater sense of purpose and meaning in our lives. Whether we realize it or not, we are all part of a Loving Consciousness. As one of my favorite poets e.e. cummings says love, *"is the wonder that's keeping the stars apart."* No one is alone. We are all on this journey together. We are operating on an energetic level which is attracting exactly what our soul needs for its spiritual development at every moment. Here are my 5 steps to help support you in discovering your life's purpose:

5 Steps to Discover Your Life Purpose:

Step 1: Trust Your Intuition

On your spiritual journey, it is important to trust yourself and follow your intuition. Have you ever gotten a feeling about something and it was right? That's your intuition! Intuition is a muscle that can be strengthened the more you use it. Acknowledge those inner inklings and nudges because they will direct you toward your life's purpose

Step 2: Follow Your Bliss

Discovering your joy will help align you with your true purpose and allow you to project that bliss out into the world. Each person's happiness is contagious and elevates humanity. This is why following your joy is a blessing that will lead you to your calling

Step 3: Discover Your Spiritual Gifts

Each of us has individual strengths and abilities which makes us unique. These talents and faculties will help you find your purpose. You have a special calling which only you can fulfill. One way to discover your inner gifts is to list the virtues and abilities you have to serve others

Step 4: Find Your Community

If you haven't already, connect with other like-minded individuals. It is said that you become like the five people you spend the most time with, therefore it is important to surround yourself with those who love and support you. Connecting with your people will empower you and give you the courage to follow your dreams

Step 5: Take Action

This is the often hardest and most exciting step to finding your life's purpose. In the #1 New York Times bestselling book *Eat Pray Love*, there is a moment when the author's mentor turns to her and says, *"if you want to get to the castle, you have to swim the moat."* Many do not even start the journey for fear of failure. The beauty of discovering your life's purpose is that there is no failure, only learning experiences which will lead you to the treasure you seek. Remember the answers are already within and you just need to listen

In the classic self-help book, *The Game of Life and How to Play It*, Florence Scovel Shinn explains that while most people consider life to be a battle, it is in fact a game of giving and receiving. Scovel Schinn describes human existence as a boomerang where every thought, word, and action we express will eventually return to us with surprising accuracy. Life is a mirror and our environment is an extension of ourselves. We cannot control what happens to us, but we can control how we react and respond. Our focus should always be on uplifting the hearts of others which will in effect raise our own vibration. This is similar to the Golden Rule that is found throughout all the major world religions, which is to treat others how we wish to be treated. Whether you adhere to a specific religion or spiritual practice or not, we are at a critical point in humanity's history where we need to respect our differences in order to coexist. In other words, loving one another is essential for our survival. Let's consider the Golden Rule across the epochs:

The Golden Rule:

Judaism
"What is hateful to you, do not to your neighbor. This is the whole Torah, all the rest is commentary" -Hillel the Elder; *Talmud*, Shabbat 31a

Christianity
"Do unto others as you would have others do unto you" -Gospel of Matthew 7:12; *NIV*

Islam
"Do unto all men as you would wish to have done unto you; and reject for others what you would reject for yourself" -Hadith

Buddhism
"Hurt not others in ways that you yourself would find hurtful" -Udana-Varga 5:18

Hinduism
"This is the sum of duty: Do naught unto others which would cause you pain if done to you" -Mahabharata 5:1517

Zoroastrianism
"Whatever is disagreeable to yourself do not do unto others" -Shayest Na-Shayest 13:29

Baha'i Faith
"He should not wish for others what he does not wish for himself" -Baha'u'llah, *Epistle to the Son of the Wolf*

Did you know that giving to others has been scientifically proven to increase happiness, improve mental and physical health, enhance connection, evoke gratitude, and is literally contagious! What's not to love? Random acts of kindness are particularly special in that we are doing something for someone we don't know and expecting nothing in return. These demonstrations often multiple and ripple out into a sea of love and kindness in the world. Here are 20 random acts of kindness ideas:

20 Random Acts of Kindness:

- pay for the person behind you in line
- leave coins on an expired parking meter
- donate to a local charity
- compliment a stranger
- bake sweets for a neighbor
- let someone go ahead of you in line
- give an extra generous tip
- donate to a food pantry
- use sidewalk chalk and write a positive message
- donate toys to a children's hospital
- participate in a charity walk or run
- give up your seat to someone
- smile and say "hello" to a stranger
- buy a gift for a foster child
- donate blood
- support a local business
- leave a positive review for a small business or lesser-known author
- donate school supplies to a disadvantaged school
- bring someone coffee or food at work
- donate books to the library

Now let's examine the 12 Universal Laws which are considered to be universal, unchanging laws that the ancient Egyptian and Hawaiian cultures were aware of. These laws cannot be created or destroyed, as they are simply observations of the workings of our universe. Their purpose is to infuse our lives with love and joy while supporting our spiritual evolution. Here are the 12 Universal Laws with present day examples:

The 12 Universal Laws:

1. *The Law of Divine Oneness*-represents the interconnectedness of humanity. Every thought, action, and event are in some way tied to everything else. Similar to the teachings of the Baha'i Faith that we are all connected (ex. asking yourself: *"How can I see the bigger picture here? How can I best use my gifts and talents? How can I fulfill my purpose and serve humanity?"*).
2. *The Law of Vibration*-everything in the universe has a unique vibrational frequency. This applies to our thoughts, feelings, and behaviors which will match with identical vibration patterns (ex. become aware of your thoughts, spend time with uplifting souls, engage in activities that bring you joy, etc.).
3. *The Law of Correspondence-"as within, so without"* or *"as above, so below."* This law notes that your external reality is a reflection of your internal state. In other words, we are in control of our lives and hold the key to our happiness (ex. if you are struggling in a particular area of your life, ask yourself what it is trying to teach you and how can you heal?).
4. *The Law of Attraction-"like attracts like."* Energy is always seeking its vibrational match and what you continually focus on will manifest itself into your life (ex. asking for what you want, believing you deserve it, and being open to receiving).

5. *The Law of Inspired Action*-when you are aligned with your authentic self, inspiration will appear and it will be easier to take inspired action. Our actions should support our personal values (ex. take a moment and hold space for your internal guidance to speak through you before making a decision).

6. *The Law of Perpetual Transmutation of Energy*-states that energy is always moving and evolving. Since every action is preceded by a thought, our thoughts create our reality. When applied with intention, higher frequencies transmute lower ones (ex. spend time with people who raise your vibration and avoid those who drain your energy).

7. *The Law of Cause and Effect*-explains that every action has a reaction and nothing happens by chance. Similar to Newton's Third Law which states that for every action force, there will be an equal and opposite reaction. This law applies to our thoughts, words, and actions (ex. taking conscious action and remembering that whatever you put out into the world will eventually be returned unto you).

8. *The Law of Compensation*-*"we reap, what we sow."* What you give to others, will be given to you and what you withhold from others will be withheld from you (ex. recognizing that you will be rewarded for your efforts and everything is working out for your highest good. You cannot lose what is meant for you. No matter what is happening, keep moving forward and trust that you will be taken care of).

9. *The Law of Relativity*-we all perceive our reality in different ways and everything is relative (ex. worrying less about being "right" and focusing more on unity).

10. *The Law of Polarity*-everything in life has an opposite and there are two sides to everything. For every challenge, there is an

opportunity and for every problem, there is a solution (ex. looking for the silver lining in a difficult situation).
11. *The Law of Rhythm*-nothing in life is permanent and everything is in flux. Cycles are a natural part of our existence. It is important to accept all stages of development and aspects of life (ex. trusting your body's natural rhythms, taking care of yourself, and resting when you need to).
12. *The Law of Gender*-living in alignment with our masculine and feminine energies (ex. balancing and integrating your masculine and feminine sides).

We will conclude this chapter by breaking down and exploring the 12 Laws of Karma. The word karma is Sanskrit for *action*. These laws are derived from the Buddhist and Hindu spiritual teachings in order for us to better comprehend how energy works and how to harness the laws to attain enlightenment. Understanding these laws can offer us a greater sense of joy, peace, and fulfillment in our lives. Keep in mind that karma is not meant to "punish" us, but rather lead us toward making positive changes and becoming our most authentic selves. Here we will examine each law along with present day examples:

The 12 Laws of Karma:

1. *The Great Law (Cause and Effect)*-whether we are conscious or not, whatever we send out into the universe will be returned to us (ex. to attract true abundance, you must be giving of your time, knowledge, and resources or to manifest love, you must be loving and compassionate with others, etc.).
2. *The Law of Creation*-life does not happen by itself and is the result of our inner state (ex. becoming an active participant in the creation of your story, surrounding yourself with things

that are supportive to your growth, using your gifts and talents to uplift the hearts of others, etc.).

3. *The Law of Humility*-one must accept something in order to change it. Taking responsibility for our lives is essential and being humble is a superpower (ex. if there is an area in your life you want to change, first accept it and stop resisting. This will pave the way for transformation).

4. *The Law of Growth*-when we change ourselves, the world around us changes. Focusing on improving our internal environment can work wonders (ex. prioritizing your personal growth, being open to endless evolution, etc.).

5. *The Law of Responsibility*-taking accountability for our thoughts and actions (ex. refusing to make excuses or blame anyone or anything else, taking responsibility for your life, etc.).

6. *The Law of Connection*-everyone and everything is connected, including the past, present, and future. No action is insignificant because it is contributing to the person you are today and who you will become (ex. practicing mindfulness, recognizing that every chapter of your story holds unique value, etc.).

7. *The Law of Focus*-we cannot think of two different things at the same time. Our intentions must be aligned with our actions since what we focus on will grow (ex. if you are focusing on spiritual values, you will have less time for lower energies such as jealousy or anger).

8. *The Law of Giving and Hospitality*-"*walking the walk.*" Our actions should reflect our deepest held beliefs (ex. if we value love, kindness, and generosity, we must demonstrate and embody these things).

9. *The Law of Change*-history repeats itself until we learn the lesson and take action (ex. attracting the same type of partner, life patterns, reoccurring struggles, etc.).

10. *The Law of Here and Now*-if we are living in the past or future, we are missing out on our lives which is always in the present moment. Old beliefs, thoughts, and behaviors prevent us from creating new ones (ex. making peace with the past, staying positive and hopeful, writing a new story, etc.).
11. *The Law of Patience and Reward*-the most valuable rewards in life require patience and persistence. Enjoy the journey and not just the destination (ex. showing up consistently and not giving up even if progress is slow, celebrating every milestone along the way, etc.).
12. *The Law of Significance and Inspiration*-your voice and your contributions matter because they make an impact in the world. You are valuable and have a unique purpose that only you can fulfill. The world of existence would not be the same without you (ex. following your bliss, listening to your intuition, honoring your dreams, etc.).

Seviana's Story Part 3

"This is so exciting! I keep manifesting things!" Seviana enthusiastically exclaimed.

My client Seviana was familiar with the law of attraction, however we took this to another level in my program together. One module is specifically dedicated to the law of attraction and how to manifest your desires into your life. Seviana was becoming more acquainted with the power of visualization and raising her energy to a higher frequency which in turn altered her external environment. She was at a concert and wanted someone to ask her to dance. Bam! A kind and attractive gentleman approached her and asked if she'd like to dance with him. She wanted deep, fulfilling, and meaningful friendships. Bam! She finally released the toxic friendships that had been holding her down and made new best friends. These days, she sends me videos of her confidently dancing with handsome men at events and appreciating all the attention. The truth was, Seviana had the magic all along. Once she believed she was worthy and deserving of incredible things, she was better able to attract them into her life. Moral of the story: we can only receive what we believe we *deserve*. Seviana now has faith in the power of her dreams. She recently manifested an amazing new job and she finally believes that she is worthy of an abundant life.

Loving the world looks like:

- Finding your life's purpose
- Following your passion
- Being who you truly are
- Spreading joy wherever you go
- Reaching out to those in need
- Complimenting others
- Being a positive role model
- Doing random acts of kindness
- Looking for the best in others
- Serving humanity

Activity #1:

My Life's Purpose

Instructions: Based on the 5 Steps to Find Your Life Purpose outlined earlier in the chapter, answer the following questions:

Step 1: Trust Your Intuition

What comes naturally to you? Are there any careers or vocations that you feel intuitively drawn to? What is it about them that resonates with you?

Step 2: Follow Your Bliss

Is there anything that excites your soul? What lights you up from the inside out?

Step 3: Discover Your Spiritual Gifts

Write down at least 5 of your virtues or spiritual strengths:

Step 4: Find Your Community

Have you found your people? If not, where do you think they are and how can you reach out?

Step 5: Take Action

What is one action step that you can take today to make your dream a reality? What is something you would do if you couldn't fail?

Activity #2:

Spread the Love

Write down 3 ways in which you can bring joy to others (ex. donating, helping others, complimenting someone, random acts of kindness, etc.). Feel free to use the Random Acts of Kindness list from before or come up with your own ideas to share your light

Activity #3:

Acts of Service

Instructions: From the list below, choose one way to serve others and your community. You can also come up with additional ways to help others:

Service Ideas:

- adopt a rescue pet
- foster dogs and cats that don't have homes
- collect pet food and supplies for an animal shelter
- become a Big Brother or Big Sister
- babysit free of charge
- mentor or tutor a student
- help an elderly neighbor with chores
- visit a nursing home or elderly facility
- create care packages with essential items for those in need
- walk a neighbor's dog
- organize a clothing drive
- create first aid kits for the homeless
- host a fundraising event
- volunteer to support children with special needs
- plant trees, flowers, or fruit in a community garden
- participate in local conservation efforts
- clean up your local park or playground (be sure to wear gloves)
- volunteer at a non-profit or shelter
- help out in a soup kitchen or food pantry
- ask for charitable donations instead of birthday or holiday gifts

Final Thoughts

We have come to end of our journey together, but your adventure my dear is only just beginning. I am so proud of you for showing up, doing the work, and making yourself a priority. It has been truly an honor and a privilege to walk alongside you on your way. This book was meant to provide you with a foundation for wholeheartedly accepting and loving yourself. Self-love is a never-ending path of connecting to your higher self and uncovering the truth of who you are. Loving yourself is a daily practice and some days will be better than others. Self-love is not always a linear path but it is a continual process. Remember to focus on your progress instead of being "perfect" because perfection does not exist. The important thing is to show yourself patience and compassion when times get tough because so are you! You are stronger, more capable, and more resilient than you know. It takes courage to be vulnerable and face our pain and struggles. Give yourself credit for doing the inner healing work and be sure to do something special to celebrate yourself. You deserve it!

As you continue to embark on your self-love quest, you may notice that you are finally able to release what is not serving you and your old limiting beliefs will eventually fade away. More than likely you will attract new people and experiences which will support your growth and development. By stepping into this empowered version of yourself, you will manifest exciting opportunities and possibilities you could have never imagined. You always hold the pen in your hand and can write a new story with yourself no longer as the victim of your past, but as the hero of your future. The dreams in your heart were planted there for a reason and now is the time to honor your deepest hopes and wishes.

The stories shared here of real women who have experienced the transformative effects of self-love demonstrate what is possible. Loving ourselves is a superpower which impacts all areas of our lives. My hope is that you have a greater awareness and acceptance of who you are, as well as your talents, strengths, and personal values which will help light the way of your journey. You now have the tools to silence your inner critic, banish self-doubt, and step into your life more confidently and empowered. You hopefully have a better understanding of the far-reaching effects of self-compassion and how speaking kindly to yourself can transform your life. We also explored the power of radical self-love which means embracing your "flaws" or "imperfections" and rejecting the need to adhere to society's unrealistic standards. Living in a world that profits off of your self-doubt and insecurities, loving yourself is a revolutionary act. This is the ultimate test of courage: being your authentic self and loving yourself every step of the way. Stand firm in the truth of who you are and do not allow the misguided opinions of others to sway you away from your destiny. You are meant to do important things in this world. Your existence has a major significance and can improve the world for us all. Always believe that you are inherently enough and deserving of all good things. By owning your power and knowing your worth, you are truly an unstoppable force of nature. When you shine your light, it gives others permission to as well. Loving yourself is a gift to the world.

Want more self-love tips and support?

Follow me on Instagram @juliaspiritualcoaching or check out my website
www.juliaspiritualcoaching.com

References

10 tips to overcome self-doubt. (2021, October 12). Eugene Therapy, https://eugenetherapy.com/article/overcome-self-doubt/

145+ community service ideas for students, families, and individuals. Fundly. (2021, June 2). https://blog.fundly.com/community-service-ideas/

Ackerman, C. E. (2022, June 20). *19 best narrative therapy techniques & worksheets [+PDF].* PositivePsychology.com, https://positivepsychology.com/narrative-therapy/

Ackerman, C. E. (2018, July 12). *What is self-acceptance? 25 exercises + definition and quotes.* PositivePsychology.com, https://positivepsychology.com/self-acceptance/

Adams, A. J. (2009, December 3). *Seeing is believing: the power of visualization.* Psychology Today, https://www.psychologytoday.com/us/blog/flourish/200912/seeing-is-believing-the-power-visualization?amp

Ali, S. (2018). *The self-love workbook: a life-changing guide to boost self-esteem, recognize your worth and find genuine happiness.* Berkeley, CA: Ulysses Press.

Anthony. (2022, April 16). *15 common cognitive distortions.* Mind My Peelings, https://www.mindmypeelings.com/blog/cognitive-distortions

Balkhi, S. (2020, May 5). *4 self-reflection tips that will make you a better person.* Thrive, https://thriveglobal.com/stories/4-self-reflection-tips-that-will-make-you-a-better-person/amp/

Battles, M. (2021, January 12). *15 ways to practice positive self-talk for success.* Lifehack, https://www.lifehack.org/504756/self-talk-determines-your-success-15-tips

Beattie, M. (1992). *Codependent no more: how to stop controlling others and start caring for yourself.* Center City, MN: Hazelden.

Beck, A. (1967). *Depression causes and treatment.* Philadelphia, PA: University of Pennsylvania Press.

Beck, J. S. (2011). *Cognitive behavior therapy: basics and beyond* (2nd ed.). New York, NY: Guilford Press.

Bloom, C. & L. (2019, September 12). *Self-trust and how to build it.* Psychology Today, https://www.psychologytoday.com/us/blog/stronger-the-broken-places/201909/self-trust-and-how-build-it?amp

Boundaries info sheet (Worksheet). (2016). Therapist Aid. https://www.therapistaid.com/therapy-worksheet/boundaries-psychoeducation-printout

Brach, T. (2004). *Radical acceptance: embracing your life with the heart of a Buddha.* New York, NY: Bantam Books.

Brady, K. (2020, November 4). *7 tips for practicing self-forgiveness.* Keir Brady Counseling Services, https://keirbradycounseling.com/self-forgiveness/

Campbell, J. (1949). *The hero with a thousand faces.* (1st ed.). Princeton, NJ: Princeton University Press.

Carpenter, K. (2020). *The empath's workbook: practical strategies for nurturing your unique gifts and living an empowered life.* Emeryville, CA: Rockbridge Press.

Chapman, G. D. (2010). *The five love languages.* Chicago, IL: Northfield Publishing.

Cherry, K. (2022, April 28). *How do you know if you're a fully functioning person?* Verywell Mind, from https://www.verywellmind.com/fully-functioning-person-2795197

Cherry, K. (2022, February 14). *What is self-concept and how does it form?* Verywell Mind. Retrieved, https://www.verywellmind.com/what-is-self-concept-2795865

Clance, P.R., & Imes, S.A. (1978). *The imposter phenomenon in high achieving women: Dynamics and therapeutic intervention.* Psychotherapy: Theory, Research & Practice, 15(3), 241.

Clance, P.R. (1985). *The impostor phenomenon: overcoming the fear that haunts your success.* Atlanta, GA: Peachtree Publishers.

Daskal, L. (2016, January 25). *35 signs you're in a toxic relationship.* Inc.com, https://www.inc.com/lolly-daskal/35-signs-youre-in-a-toxic-business-relationship.html

Davis, D. E., Ho, M. Y., Griffin, B. J., Bell, C., Hook, J. N., Van Tongeren, D. R., DeBlaere, C., Worthington, E. L., Jr., & Westbrook, C. J. (2015). *Forgiving the self and physical and mental health correlates: A meta-analytic review.* Journal of Counseling Psychology, 62(2), 329–335. https://doi.org/10.1037/cou0000063

Desjardins, J. (2021, November 29). *24 cognitive biases that are warping your perception of reality.* Visual Capitalist, https://www.visualcapitalist.com/24-cognitive-biases-warping-reality/

Dsouza, M. (2020, November 20). *Cognitive biases - the complete guide - types, tips, examples.* Productive Club, https://productiveclub.com/cognitive-biases/?q=decision-making

Dweck, C.S. (2008). *Mindset: the new psychology of success.* Random House Digital, Inc. https://psycnet.apa.org/record/2006-08575-000

Estrada, J. (2022, June 28). *12 laws of karma: what are they and how do they affect you?* Well+Good, https://www.wellandgood.com/12-laws-of-karma/amp/

Eurich, T. (2019). *What self-awareness really is (and how to cultivate it).* [online] Harvard Business Review, https://hbr.org/2018/01/what-self-awareness-really-is-and-how-to-cultivate-it

Evans, R.R. (@ryanroseevans). (2021, October 27). *Trauma responses.* Instagram, https://www.instagram.com/p/CVjz0QzBICz/?igshid=NzNkNDdiOGI=

Faherty, M. (2016, August 9). *Why spend time working on self-advocacy skills? (part 1).* Rule The School, https://rule-the-school.com/2016/08/09/why-spend-time-working-on-self-advocacy-skills-part-1/amp/

Gardner, H. (1983). *Frames of mind: the theory of multiple intelligences.* New York, NY: Basic Books.

Gardner, H. (2006). *Multiple intelligences: new horizons.* New York, NY: Basic Books.

Gilbert, E. (2006). *Eat, Pray, Love.* New York, NY: Viking Press.

Golden Rule. (2020, July 18). *New World Encyclopedia,* https://www.newworldencyclopedia.org/p/index.php?title=Golden_Rule&oldid=1039683.

Goleman, D. (1995). *Emotional intelligence: why it can matter more than IQ*. New York, NY: Bantam Book.

Hall, K. (2014, July 12). *Self-validation*. Psychology Today, https://www.psychologytoday.com/us/blog/pieces-mind/201407/self-validation?amp

Hallman, C. (2021, December 13). *50 cognitive biases to be aware of so you can be the very best version of you*. TitleMax, https://www.titlemax.com/discovery-center/lifestyle/50-cognitive-biases-to-be-aware-of-so-you-can-be-the-very-best-version-of-you/

Harrington, R. & Loffredo, D. A. (2010). *Insight, rumination, and self-reflection as predictors of well-being*. The Journal of Psychology, 145:1, 39-57, DOI: 10.1080/00223980.2010.528072

Jackman, R. (2020). *Healing your lost inner child: how to stop impulse reactions, set healthy boundaries and embrace an authentic life*. USA: Practical Wisdom Press.

Jenev Caddell, P. D. (2020, September 17). *5 differences between coaching and psychotherapy*. Verywell Mind, https://www.verywellmind.com/should-i-work-with-a-psychotherapist-or-coach-2337587

Johari Window: Model and Free Diagrams. (n.d.). BusinessBalls.com, https://www.businessballs.com/self-awareness/johari-window-model-and-free-diagrams/

Jovanović, S. P. (2021, September 22). *Self-validation: 5 ways to develop it*. happiness.com, https://www.happiness.com/magazine/science-psychology/self-validation/

Jung, C. G. (1921). *Psychological types. the collected works of C. G. Jung*, Vol. 6, Bollingen Series XX.

Jung, C. G., & Carrington, H. R. F. (1993). *Psychology and alchemy*. Princeton, NJ: Princeton University Press.

Jung, C. G., & Carrington, H. R. F. (1990). *The archetypes and the collective unconscious*. Princeton, NJ: Princeton University Press.

Kamiya, M. (1979). *Ikigai ni tsuite*. Misuzu Shobō.

Katherine. (2020, October 21). *How to develop self-trust.* Life Coach Directory, https://www.lifecoach-directory.org.uk/blog/2020/10/22/how-to-develop-self-trust

Kooiman-Cox, L. (2022, February 14). *8 types of self-care.* Willowstone Family Services. https://www.willowstone.org/news/8-types-of-self-care

Kosik, A. H. (2018, March 13). *11 expert tips to help put an end to self-judgments.* brit, https://www.brit.co/amp/how-to-stop-self-judgments-2639473403

Krznaric, R. (2020, December 7). *The ancient greeks' 6 words for love (and why knowing them can change your life).* YES! Magazine, https://www.yesmagazine.org/health-happiness/2013/12/28/the-ancient-greeks-6-words-for-love-and-why-knowing-them-can-change-your-life

Lebowitz, S. (2015, August 26). *20 cognitive biases that screw up your decisions.* Business Insider, https://www.businessinsider.com/cognitive-biases-that-affect-decisions-2015-8

Lemola, S., Räikkönen, K., Gomez, V. et al. (2013). *Optimism and self-esteem are related to sleep: results from a large community-based sample.* International Journal of Behavioral Medicine, 20, 567–571. https://doi.org/10.1007/s12529-012-9272-z

Levine, A. and Heller, R. (2011). *Attached the new science of adult attachment and how it can help you find-and keep-love.* New York, NY: Penguin Random House.

Logan, M. (2020). *Self-love workbook for women: release self-doubt, build self-compassion, and embrace who you are.* Emeryville, CA: Rockridge Press.

Lopez-Garrido, G. (2020, September 13). *Locus of control.* Simply Psychology, https://www.simplypsychology.org/locus-of-control.html

Love your body: 10 tips for body positivity. (2019, October 22). Center For Discovery: Eating Disorder Treatment, https://centerfordiscovery.com/blog/10-tips-body-positivity/

Luft, J. & Ingham, H. (1955). *The Johari window, a graphic model of interpersonal awareness, proceedings of the western training laboratory in group development.* Los Angeles: UCLA.

Manz, C. C. (1983). *Improving performance through self-leadership.* National Productivity Review, 2(3), 288–297.

Marlene, C. (2019, December 2). *30 day kindness challenge (random acts of kindness).* Cydney Marlene, https://cydneymarlene.com/2019/12/30-day-kindness-challenge/

Marsh, J. & Suttie, J. (2010, December 18). *5 ways giving is good for you.* Greater Good, https://greatergood.berkeley.edu/article/item/5_ways_giving_is_good_for_you

Martin, S. (2021, September 24). *Benefits of setting boundaries: why you need to set healthy boundaries.* Live Well with Sharon Martin, https://www.livewellwithsharonmartin.com/6-benefits-of-setting-boundaries/

Martin, S. (2018, December 21). *Why we abandon ourselves and how to stop.* Psych Central, https://psychcentral.com/blog/imperfect/2018/12/why-we-abandon-ourselves-and-how-to-stop#How-to-stop-abandoning-yourself

Maslow, A. H. (1970). *Motivation and personality* (2nd ed.). New York, NY: Harper & Row.

McDuff, K. (2022, May 26). *7 examples of self-awareness in everyday life: What is self-awareness.* My Question Life, https://myquestionlife.com/examples-of-self-awareness-in-everyday-life/

Mcleod, S. (2020, December 29). *Maslow's hierarchy of needs.* Simply Psychology, https://www.simplypsychology.org/maslow.html

Mead, E. (2022, August 20). *What is positive self-talk?* (incl. examples). PositivePsychology.com, https://positivepsychology.com/positive-self-talk/

Meyers, N. (2006). *The holiday.* Sony Pictures Releasing.

Minuchin, S. (1974). *Families and family therapy.* Cambridge, MA: Harvard University Press.

Moore, M. (2021, November 11). *Narcissist and codependent compatibility in relationships.* Psych Central, https://psychcentral.com/disorders/the-dance-between-codependents-narcissists#codependency

Multiple intelligences test. (n.d.). IDRlabs, https://www.idrlabs.com/multiple-intelligences/test.php

Neff, K. (2015). *Self-compassion: the proven power of being kind to yourself.* New York, NY: Harper Collins.

Neuhaus, M. (2022, August 21). *Developing self-leadership: your ultimate coaching guide.* PositivePsychology.com, https://positivepsychology.com/developing-self-leadership/

Neuhaus, M. N. (2022, August 20). *What is self-leadership? models, theory and examples.* PositivePsychology.com, https://positivepsychology.com/self-leadership/

Nguyen, J. (2021, September 11). *Fight, flight, freeze, fawn: examining the 4 trauma responses.* mindbodygreen, https://www.mindbodygreen.com/articles/fight-flight-freeze-fawn-trauma-responses

Nguyen, S. O. (2022, July 1). *These 33 self-acceptance tips will help you love yourself as you are.* Parade, https://parade.com/.amp/1227716/stephnguyen/self-acceptance/

Orloff, J. (2020). *The empath's survival guide: life strategies for sensitive people.* Boulder, CO: Sounds True.

Our Mindful Life. (2022, April 19). *What is the meaning and benefits of self-love.* Our Mindful Life, https://www.ourmindfullife.com/self-love-benefits/

Page, O. (2020, November 4). *How to leave your comfort zone and enter your 'growth zone'.* PositivePsychology.com, https://positivepsychology.com/comfort-zone/

Peterson, T.J. (2021, May 31). *Self-sabotaging: why we do it & 8 ways to stop.* Choosing Therapy, https://www.choosingtherapy.com/self-sabotaging/#how-to-stop-self-sabotaging-8-tips

Phooi, M. (2021, September 23). *12 universal laws.* First Media Design School, https://firstmedia.edu.sg/self-development/12-universal-laws/

Popov, L.K. (2000). *The virtues project: simple ways to create a culture of character: educator's guide.* Fawnskin, CA: Jalmar Press

Regan, S. (2021, July 21). *12 universal laws & how to use them to unlock a more spiritual life.* Mindbodygreen, https://amp.mindbodygreen.com/articles/the-12-universal-laws-and-how-to-practice-them

Rekhi, S. (n.d.). *Self-acceptance: definition, quotes, & how to practice it*. The Berkeley Well-Being Institute, https://www.berkeleywellbeing.com/self-acceptance.html

Resnick, B. (2020, June 22). *"Reality" is constructed by your brain. here's what that means, and why it matters*. Vox, https://www.vox.com/platform/amp/science-and-health/20978285/optical-illusion-science-humility-reality-polarization

Rickett, M. (2020, April 20). *How to use the hero's journey to craft the perfect screenplay*. StudioBinder, https://www.studiobinder.com/blog/joseph-campbells-heros-journey/#Call-to-Action

Rogers, C. R. (1959). *A theory of therapy, personality, and interpersonal relationships as developed in the client-centered framework*. Psychology: A Story of a Science, Vol. 3, edited by Sigmund Koch, McGraw-Hill, pp. 184-256.

Rogers, C. R. (1963). *The concept of the fully functioning person*. Psychotherapy: Theory, Research & Practice, *1*(1), 17–26. https://doi.org/10.1037/h0088567

Rotter, J. B. (1954). *Social learning and clinical psychology*. Prentice-Hall, Inc. https://doi.org/10.1037/10788-000

Rowling, J. K. (2007). *Harry potter and the deathly hallows*. New York, NY: Arthur A. Levine Books.

Ruhl, C. (2021, May 4). *What is cognitive bias?* Simply Psychology, https://www.simplypsychology.org/cognitive-bias.html#examples

Senninger, T. (2000). *Abenteuer leiten – in abenteuern lernen*. Münster: Ökotopia.

Shinn, F. S. (1925). *The game of life and how to play it*. Camarillo, CA: DeVorss

Smith, J. (2020, September 25). *Growth mindset vs fixed mindset: how what you think affects what you achieve*. Mindset Health, https://www.mindsethealth.com/matter/growth-vs-fixed-mindset

Spector, N. (2019, November 6). *What is self-awareness? and how can you cultivate it?* NBCNews.com, https://www.nbcnews.com/better/amp/ncna1067721

Srivastava, I. T. (2020, October 18). *You can change your life by applying these 12 laws of karma.* Medium, https://medium.com/be-unique/you-can-change-your-life-by-applying-these-12-laws-of-karma-681c2d27674e

St. John, N. (2017, December 6). *Why your mind is like an iceberg.* HuffPost. https://www.huffpost.com/entry/why-your-mind-is-like-an-_b_6285584/amp

Stead, H. J. (2019, October 22). *4 carl jung theories explained: persona, shadow, anima/ animus, the self.* Medium, https://medium.com/personal-growth/4-carl-jung-theories-explained-persona-shadow-anima-animus-the-self-4ab6df8f7971

The Teaching Factor. (2017, September 24). *The hero's journey: a study in film.* The Teaching Factor, https://theteachingfactor.wordpress.com/2017/09/24/the-heros-journey-a-study-in-film/

The Trustees of Princeton University. (n.d.). *Understanding your communication style* | Umatter. Princeton University, https://umatter.princeton.edu/respect/tools/communication-styles

Vidor, King, et al. (1939). *The Wizard of Oz.* Metro-Goldwyn-Mayer (MGM).

What is self advocacy. (2017, November 23). Selfadvocatenet.com, https://selfadvocatenet.com/what-is-self-advocacy/

What is self-care? self-care and mental health. (n.d.) YoungMinds, https://www.youngminds.org.uk/young-person/coping-with-life/self-care/

What is your self-care language? Take the self-love language quiz. (2021, November 25), https://findingjulianne.com/self-love-language-quiz/

Williamson, M. (1992). *A course in miracles.* Mill Valley, CA: Foundation for Inner Peace.

Wolf, N. (1991). *The beauty myth.* New York, NY: Harper Collins.

Wong, K. (2022, June 21). *12 universal laws: how to use them.* The Millennial Grind, https://millennial-grind.com/the-12-laws-of-the-universe-explained/

Woodard, J. (@_jakewoodard). (2022, August 4). *Inner child wounds.* Instagram, https://www.instagram.com/p/Cg2CB9iuCX5/?igshid=NzNkNDdiOGI=

Yang, S. (2022, July 29). *12 signs of a healthy relationship, according to therapists.* TheThirty, https://thethirty.whowhatwear.com/signs-of-a-healthy-relationship/slide2

Index

12 Laws of Karma, 162, 169-171
12 Universal Laws, 162, 166-168

affirmations, 67, 73, 78, 135
alchemy, 21
Angelou, Maya, 74
anxiety, 11, 22, 51, 53, 71, 74, 85, 91, 103, 118, 121, 140
Aristotle, 117
Attached (Levine & Heller), 90-91
attachment styles, 81, 90-91
attachment theory, 90
authenticity, 3, 9, 12, 14, 28, 49-50, 53, 96, 111, 117-118, 122-123, 128, 167, 169, 176

Baha'i, 15, 165-166
Baha'u'llah, 165
Ball, Lucille, 5
Beattie, Melody, 92
Beauty Myth (the), 59-60
Beck, Aaron, 35
Bible (the), 17, 164
blind spots, 33, 38-39, 41, 149
body acceptance, 57, 59-61
body image, 3, 11, 17, 24, 60, 62, 68, 83, 87, 111
body positivity, 57, 59
boundaries, 3, 12, 19, 30, 63, 84-85, 87, 92-93, 101-109, 112, 114-115, 132, 136, 139, 141
Brach, Tara, 52
Brady, Keir, 75-78
Buddhism, 8, 52, 165, 168
burnout, 103-104, 132, 134, 137

Campbell, Joseph, 15, 45
Chapman, Gary, 135
Clance, Pauline, 119-121

codependency, 44, 81, 84-85, 92-93
cognitive biases, 29, 32-35
cognitive distortions, 29, 32, 35-37, 46
comfort zone, 12, 24, 29, 42-43, 118, 160
common humanity, 9-10, 20, 67-69, 75, 162
communication, 1, 81, 92, 95, 104, 108, 110, 141, 149
coping skills, 133-134, 142, 154
cummings, e.e., 162

depression, 11, 22, 44, 51, 53, 71, 74, 91, 118, 140
DiClemente, Carol, 153-155
DiLeonardo, Madeleine, 96
divine feminine energy, 118, 123-125
Dweck, Carol, 146-147

Eat Pray Love book, 163
emotional health, 7-8, 11, 51, 54, 56-57, 74, 91, 93, 103, 131, 133-134, 138, 140
emotional intelligence, 29, 39-40, 56
emotions wheel, 80
empath, 133, 140-142
Epston, David, 96-98
Eurich, Tasha, 38-39
Evans, Ryan Rose, 85

Five Love Languages (the) book, 135
Ford, Henry, 72
Frohman, Denise, 81

Game of Life (the) book, 164
Gardner, Howard, 145, 148-149
golden rule, 162, 164-165
Goleman, Daniel, 39
growth mindset, 146-147
growth zone, 42-43

Harry Potter and the Deathly Hallows film, 28
Healing Your Lost Inner Child book, 82-83
hero's journey, 15-21, 24, 86, 96
hierarchy of needs (Maslow), 155-157
Hinduism, 165, 168
Huxley, Aldous, 145

ikigai, 25-26
Imes, Suzanne, 119-121
imposter syndrome, 118-121
Ingham, Harrington, 149-150
inner child, 41, 81-84, 87, 89-90, 149
inner critic, 2, 11, 20, 29-30, 32, 66, 98, 106, 118, 134, 176
insecurities, 12, 16, 18, 23, 29, 41, 51, 59-60, 65, 83, 86, 93, 101, 118, 120, 176
intuition, 10, 40, 78, 108, 124, 133, 142, 149, 162, 171-172
Islam, 164

Jackman, Robert, 82-83
Johari Window, 146, 149-150
Judaism, 164
Jung, Carl, 15, 24, 29, 39-41, 49, 82-83

Kamiya, Mieko, 25-26
Kornfield, Jack, 65

life purpose, 24-26, 159, 162, 164, 172-173

limiting beliefs, 5-6, 16, 30-31, 33, 37, 41, 72, 81-83, 86, 88-89, 91, 93, 97-99, 111-113, 175
locus of control, 118, 126-127
Logan, Megan, 93
Luft, Joseph, 149-150

main character energy, 15, 118, 125-126, 128
Manz, Charles, 150
Martin, Sharon, 103
Maslow, Abraham, 155-158
mental health, 7, 11, 17, 35, 56, 74, 103, 132-134, 140, 165
mindfulness, 28, 52, 54, 56, 66-69, 78, 134, 151, 170
Morley, Robert, 7
motivation, 11, 68, 118, 151, 157
multiple intelligences, 145, 148-149

Namdeo, Nitin, 13
narcissist, 92, 111, 141
narrative psychology/therapy, 79, 81, 96-98
Neff, Kristin, 67-70
Neuhaus, Maike, 152
Newtons Third Law, 167-168

O'Neill, Rachel, 96
Orloff, Judith, 141
overthinking, 9, 122, 140

Peck, M. Scott, 161
people-pleasing, 3, 30, 41, 50, 53, 61, 82-85, 92, 102, 107, 132, 137
perfectionism, 3, 22, 49, 61, 83, 85-86, 106, 120
Peterson, Tanya, 106-107
physical health, 7, 11, 35, 74, 103-104, 131, 134, 138, 140, 165
Popov, Linda Kavelin, 14
positive self-talk, 11, 67, 71-72, 106-107, 113, 135

Prochaska, James, 153-155

radical self-acceptance, 51-52
radical self-love, 41, 85, 176
random acts of kindness, 165-166, 173
reframing, 67, 71, 78-79, 106, 134
relationship red flags, 94
relationships, 90-97
resilience, 11, 20, 31, 46, 68, 71, 73, 134, 175
Rogers, Carl, 51, 57, 59
Roosevelt, Eleanor, 101
Rotter, Julian, 118, 126-127

self-abandonment, 51-54
self-actualization, 43, 59, 146, 155-158
self-advocacy, 102, 110-111
self-awareness archetypes, 29, 38-39
self-care:
empath, 133, 140-142
types, 133, 138-140
self-compassion break, 69-70
self-doubt, 6, 11, 16, 29-31, 41, 59, 65, 71, 85, 108, 118-120, 127, 176
self-efficacy, 12, 43, 118
self-esteem, 53, 69
self-forgiveness, 74-78
self-image, 57-58, 62, 118
self-judgement, 29, 51, 54-55
self-leadership, 146, 150-152
self-love:
benefits, 11-12

languages, 135-136
myths, 7-10
self-kindness, 9, 54, 61, 66-68, 70, 120
self-nurturing, 133, 135
self-patience, 55
self-reflection, 146, 152-153
self-sabotage, 76, 86, 106, 111-112
self-trust, 84, 108, 121-122
self-validation, 56
Senninger, Tom, 42
service ideas, 173-174
shadow work, 29, 41, 149
Shinn, Florence Scovel, 164
stages of change (model), 146, 153-155

The Holiday (movie), 117
trauma responses, 85
triggers, 18, 20, 44-45, 47, 55, 66, 72, 76-77, 120
Tugaleva, Vironika, 27

unconscious, 24, 28-29, 32, 40-41, 44, 72, 82-83, 88-89, 106, 111-112, 152
unrequited love, 93

White, Michael, 96-98
Williamson, Marianne, 112
Wizard of Oz (the) film, 101
Wolf, Naomi, 59-60
Woodard, Jake, 84

Zoroastrianism, 165

Printed in Great Britain
by Amazon